Status and Trends of Wetlands in the Conterminous United States 1998 to 2004

I0500418

T. E. Dahl
U.S. Fish and Wildlife Service
Fisheries and Habitat Conservation
Washington, D.C.

Acknowledgments

Many agencies, organizations, and individuals contributed their time, energy, and expertise to the completion of this report. The author would like to specifically recognize the following individuals for their contributions. From the Fish and Wildlife Service:
Dr. Benjamin Tuggle, John Cooper, Herb Bergquist, Jim Dick, Jonathan Hall[1], Bill Pearson, Becky Stanley[2], Dr. Mamie Parker, Everett Wilson, Jill Parker, Robin Nims Elliott. From the U.S. Geological Survey: Greg Allord, Dave McCulloch, Mitch Bergeson, Jane Harner, Liz Ciganovich, Marta Anderson, Dick Vraga, Tim Saultz, Mike Duncan, Ron Keeler and the staff of the Advanced Systems Center. From the National Park Service–Cumberland Island National Seashore: Ginger Cox, Ron Crawford and George Lewis. From the Interagency Field Team: Sally Benjamin, USDA–Farm Services Agency; Patricia Delgado, NOAA, National Marine Fisheries Service; Dr. Jeff Goebel and Daryl Lund, USDA–Natural Resources Conservation Service; David Olsen, U.S. Army Corps of Engineers; and Myra Price, U.S. Environmental Protection Agency.

Peer review of the manuscript was provided by the following technical experts: Ms. Peg Bostwick, Michigan Dept. of Environmental Quality, Lansing, MI; Dr. Ken Burham, Statistician, Department of Fishery and Wildlife Biology, Colorado State University, Fort Collins, CO; Mr. Marvin Hubbell, U.S. Army Corps of Engineers, Rock Island, IL; Mr. William Knapp, Deputy Science Advisor, U.S. Fish and Wildlife Service, Arlington, VA; Ms. Janet Morlan, Oregon Dept. of State Lands, Salem, OR; Dr. N. Scott Urquhart Research Scientist, Department of Statistics, Colorado State University, Fort Collins, CO; Mr. Joel Wagner, Hydrologist, National Park Service, Denver, CO; Dr. Dennis Whigham, Senior Scientist, Smithsonian Environmental Research Center, Edgewater, MD; Dr. Joy Zedler, Professor of Botany and Aldo Leopold Chair in Restoration Ecology, University of Wisconsin, Madison, WI.

This report is the culmination of technical collaboration and partnerships. A more complete listing of some of the cooperators appears at the end of this report.

Publication design and layout of the report were done by the Cartography and Publishing Program, U.S. Geological Survey, Madison, Wisconsin.

Photographs are by Thomas Dahl unless otherwise noted.

This report should be cited as follows:
Dahl, T.E. 2006. Status and trends of wetlands in the conterminous United States 1998 to 2004. U.S. Department of the Interior; Fish and Wildlife Service, Washington, D.C. 112 pp.

[1] Retired.
[2] Current affiliation: NOAA, National Marine Fisheries Service.

Opposite page: Louisiana, 2005.

Previous, title page: Freshwater wetland in the southeast U.S., 2005.

Tundra swans (Cygnus columbianus) and other waterfowl congregate in the freshwater marshes along the upper Mississippi River. Photo courtesy of FWS.

Funding for this study was provided by the following agencies:

Environmental Protection Agency

Department of Agriculture
Farm Services Administration
Natural Resources Conservation Service

Department of Commerce
National Marine Fisheries Service

Department of the Army
Army Corps of Engineers

Department of Interior
Fish and Wildlife Service

The Council of Environmental Quality has coordinated these interagency efforts.

A freshwater emergent wetland in Nebraska, 2005.

Preface

On Earth Day 2004, President Bush unveiled a new policy for our nation's wetlands. Moving beyond "no net loss" of wetlands, the President challenged the nation to increase the quantity as well as quality of these important resources, and set a goal of restoring, improving and protecting more than 3 million acres in five years.

The President recognized that a continuous effort to track progress toward achieving the various aspects of the Administration's new policies would be important. The Fish and Wildlife Service was in a unique position to provide the nation with sound scientific information assessing trends in the quantity of wetland gains and losses. As part of that same 2004 Earth Day message, the President directed the Service to accelerate the completion of this study and report the results.

This is the Administration's report to Congress that provides the nation with scientific and statistical results on progress made toward our national wetlands acreage goals. I am pleased to report that the nation is making excellent progress in meeting these wetland goals. For the first time net wetland gains, achieved through the contributions of restoration and creation activities, surpassed net wetland losses. This is the result of a multitude of governmental, corporate and private partnerships working together to secure and conserve our wetland resources for future generations.

This report does not draw conclusions regarding trends in the quality of the nation's wetlands. The Status and Trends Study collects data on wetland acreage gains and losses, as it has for the past 50 years. However, it is timely to examine the quality, function, and condition of such wetland acreage. Such an examination will be undertaken by agencies participating in the President's Wetlands Initiative.

Secretary, Department of the Interior

Conversion Table

U.S. Customary to Metric

inches (in.)	x	25.40	=	millimeters (mm)
inches (in.)	x	2.54	=	centimeters (cm)
feet (ft)	x	0.30	=	meters (m)
miles (mi)	x	1.61	=	kilometers (km)
nautical miles (nmi)	x	1.85	=	kilometers (km)
square feet (ft²)	x	0.09	=	square meters (m²)
square miles (mi²)	x	2.59	=	square kilometers (km²)
acres (A)	x	0.40	=	hectares (ha)
Fahrenheit degrees (F)	$\rightarrow$	0.556 (F - 32)	=	Celsius degrees (C)

Metric to U.S. Customary

millimeters (mm)	x	0.04	=	inches (in.)
centimeters (cm)	x	0.39	=	feet (ft)
meters (m)	x	3.28	=	feet (ft)
kilometers (km)	x	0.62	=	miles (mi)
square meters (m²)	x	10.76	=	square feet (ft²)
square kilometers (km²)	x	0.39	=	square miles (mi²)
hectares (ha)	x	2.47	=	acres (A)
Celsius degrees (C)	$\rightarrow$	1.8 (C) + 32)	=	Fahrenheit degrees (F)

General Disclaimer

The use of trade, product, industry or firm names or products in this report is for informative purposes only and does not constitute an endorsement by the U.S. Government or the Fish and Wildlife Service.

Contents

List of Figures

List of Tables

Opposite page: Freshwater wetlands of the Yosemite Valley, California.

Executive Summary

For over half a century the Fish and Wildlife Service has been monitoring wetland trends of the nation. In 1956, the first report on wetland status and classification provided indications that wetland habitat for migratory waterfowl had experienced substantial declines (Shaw and Fredine 1956).

Over the intervening 51 years, the Fish and Wildlife Service has implemented a scientifically based process to periodically measure wetland status and trends in the conterminous United States. The Fish and Wildlife Service's Wetlands Status and Trends study was developed specifically for monitoring the nation's wetland area using a single, consistent definition and study protocol. The Fish and Wildlife Service has specialized knowledge of wetland habitats, classification, and ecological changes and has used that capability to conduct a series of wetland monitoring studies that document the status and trends of our nation's wetlands. This report is the latest in that series of scientific studies.

Data collected for the 1998 to 2004 Status and Trends Report has led to the conclusion that for the first time net wetland gains, acquired through the contributions of restoration and creation activities, surpassed net wetland losses. There was a net gain of 191,750 wetland acres (77,630 ha) nationwide which equates to an average annual net gain of 32,000 acres (12,900 ha).

The efforts to monitor wetland status and trends that are described in this report have been enhanced by the multi-agency involvement in the study's design, data collection, verification, and peer review of the findings. Interagency funding was essential to the successful and timely completion of the study.

A freshwater forested wetland of the Great Lakes region, 2005.

The first statistical wetlands status and trends report (Frayer *et al.* 1983) estimated the rate of wetland loss between the mid 1950s and the mid 1970s at 458,000 acres (185,400 ha) per year. There have been dramatic changes since that era when wetlands were largely thought of as a hindrance to development. The first indications of those changes came from the Fish and Wildlife Service's updated status and trends report (Dahl and Johnson 1991) covering the mid 1970s to the mid 1980s. The estimated rate of wetland loss had declined to 290,000 acres (117,400 ha) per year.

In 2000, the Fish and Wildlife Service produced the third national status and trends report documenting changes that occurred between 1986 and 1997. Findings from that report indicated the annual loss rate was 58,500 acres (23,700 ha), an eighty percent reduction in the average annual rate of wetland loss.

On Earth Day 2004, President Bush announced a wetlands initiative that established a federal policy beyond "no net loss" of wetlands. The policy seeks to attain an overall increase in the quality and quantity of wetlands. The President set a goal of restoring, improving and protecting more than 3 million acres (1.2 million ha) in five years. To continue tracking wetland acreage trends, the President further directed the Fish and Wildlife Service to complete an updated wetlands status and trends study in 2005. This latest report provides the nation with scientific and statistical results on the progress that has been made toward achieving national wetland quantity goals. This report does not assess the quality or condition of the nation's wetlands. The Status and Trends Study collects data on wetland acreage gains and losses,

15

as it has for the past 50 years. However, it is timely to examine the quality, function, and condition of such wetland acreage. Such an examination will be undertaken by agencies participating in the President's Wetlands Initiative.

This study measured wetland trends in the conterminous United States between 1998 and 2004. The estimates of estuarine emergent area were made prior to Hurricanes Katrina and Rita during the summer of 2005. The Cowardin *et al.* (1979) wetland definition was used to describe wetland types. By design, intertidal wetlands of the Pacific coast, reefs and submerged aquatic vegetation were excluded from this study.

An interagency group of statisticians developed the design for the national status and trends study. The study design consisted of 4,682 randomly selected sample plots. Each plot is four square miles (2,560 acres or 1,040 ha) in area. These plots were examined, with the use of recent remotely sensed data in combination with field work, to determine wetland change. Field verification was completed for 1,504 (32 percent) of the sample plots distributed in 35 states. Representatives from four states and seven federal agencies participated in field reconnaissance trips.

Estimates were made of wetland area by wetland type and changes over time.

National Status and Trends

This study found that there were an estimated 107.7 million acres (43.6 million ha) of wetlands in the conterminous United States in 2004. Ninety-five percent of the wetlands were freshwater wetlands and five percent were estuarine or marine wetlands.

In the estuarine system, estuarine emergents dominated, making up an estimated 73 percent (almost 3.9 million acres or 1.6 million ha) of all estuarine and marine wetlands. Estuarine shrub wetlands made up 13 percent of the area and non-vegetated saltwater wetlands 14 percent.

In the freshwater system, forested wetlands made up 51 percent of the total area, the single largest freshwater category. Freshwater emergents made up an estimated 25.5 percent of the total area, shrub wetlands 17 percent and freshwater ponds 6.5 percent.

Wetland area increased by an average 32,000 acres (12,900 ha.) annually. The net gain in wetland area was attributed to wetlands created, enhanced or restored through regulatory and nonregulatory restoration programs. These gains in wetland area occurred on active agricultural lands, inactive agricultural lands, and other lands. Freshwater wetland losses to silviculture, urban and rural development offset some gains. Urban and rural development combined accounted for an estimated 61 percent of the net freshwater wetlands lost between 1998 and 2004. This study reports on changes in wetland acreage and does not provide an assessment of wetland functions or quality.

Intertidal Estuarine and Marine Wetland Resources

Three major categories of estuarine and marine wetlands were included in this study: estuarine intertidal emergents (salt and brackish water marshes), estuarine shrub wetlands (mangrove swamps) and estuarine and marine intertidal non-vegetated wetlands. This latter category included exposed coastal beaches subject to tidal flooding, shallow water sand bars, tidal flats, tidally exposed shoals, and sand spits.

In 2004, it was estimated there were slightly more than 5.3 million acres (2.15 million ha) of marine and estuarine wetlands in the conterminous United States. Estuarine emergent wetlands declined by 0.9 percent. The average annual rate of estuarine emergent loss was 5,540 acres (2,240 ha). This rate of loss was consistent with the rate of salt marsh loss recorded from 1986 to 1997. Most of the losses of estuarine emergent wetland were due to loss to deep salt water and occurred in coastal Louisiana. One or more of several interrelated factors may have contributed to these losses including: deficiencies in sediment deposition, canals and artificially created waterways, wave erosion, land subsidence, and salt water intrusion causing marsh disintegration.

There were an estimated 728,540 acres (294,960 ha) of intertidal non-vegetated wetlands in 2004. From 1998 to 2004 marine intertidal beaches declined by 1,870 acres (760 ha). Intertidal non-vegetated wetland changes to urban and other forms of upland development were statistically insignificant in this study.

There were an estimated 682,200 acres (276,190 ha) of estuarine shrub wetland in 2004. This estimate represented a small gain of about 800 acres (320 ha). The area of estuarine shrub wetlands has been steady over the past two decades.

Freshwater Wetland Resources

Large shifts between the freshwater wetland types and uplands took place between 1998 and 2004. Freshwater wetland gains resulted from restorations and the creation of numerous freshwater ponds.

Agricultural conservation programs were responsible for most of the gross wetland restoration. These gains came from lands in "agriculture" category as well as from conservation lands in the "other" land use category. Agricultural programs that promoted pond construction also contributed to the increased freshwater pond acreage.

Ponds were included as freshwater wetlands consistent with the Cowardin *et al.* definition. Freshwater pond acreage increased by almost 700,000 acres (281,500 ha) from 1998 to 2004, a 12.6 percent increase in area. This was the largest percent increase in area, of any wetland type in this study. Without the increased pond acreage, wetland gains would not have surpassed wetland losses during the timeframe of this study. The creation of artificial freshwater ponds has played a major role in achieving wetland quantity objectives. The replacement of vegetated wetland areas with ponds represents a change in wetland classification. Some freshwater ponds would not be expected to provide the same range of wetland values and functions as a vegetated freshwater wetland.

Freshwater forested wetlands were affected by two processes, the *conversion* of forested wetland to and from other wetland types through cutting or the maturation of trees, and *loss* of forested wetland where wetland hydrology was destroyed. Estimates indicated that the area of freshwater forested wetland increased. Between 1998 and 2004, forested wetland area increased by an estimated 548,200 acres (221,950 ha). Most of these changes came from small trees, previously classified as wetland shrubs, maturing and being re-classified as forest.

Despite the net gains realized from restoration and creation projects, human induced wetland losses continued to affect the trends of freshwater vegetated wetlands— especially freshwater emergent marshes which declined by an estimated 142,570 acres (57,720 ha). These wetlands are important to a number of wildlife species. Contributed inserts to the report highlight the importance of wetlands to fish and wildlife.

American avocets (Recurvirostra americana) at Bear River, Migratory Bird Refuge, Utah, a river delta wetland that attracts hundreds of species of waterfowl and shorebirds. Photo courtesy of the FWS.

Introduction

The mission of the Fish and Wildlife Service is to conserve, protect, and enhance fish, wildlife, plants, and their habitats for the continuing benefit of the American people. The Fish and Wildlife Service supports programs relating to migratory birds, endangered species, certain marine mammals, inland sport fisheries and a system of 545 national wildlife refuges. The Fish and Wildlife Service communicates information essential for public awareness and understanding of the importance of fish and wildlife resources and changes in environmental conditions that can affect the welfare of Americans. To this end, the Fish and Wildlife Service maintains an active role in monitoring wetland habitats of the nation.

The importance of wetlands as fish and wildlife habitat has always been the primary focus of the Fish and Wildlife Service's wetland activities. Wetlands are transitional from truly aquatic habitats to upland and as a result, wetland abundance, type and quality are directly reflected in the health and abundance of many fish and wildlife species.

The Emergency Wetlands Resources Act (Public Law 99-645) requires the Fish and Wildlife Service to produce national wetlands status and trend reports for the Congress at ten year intervals. The Fish and Wildlife Service has responded to this mandate with national wetlands status and trends reports in 1983, 1991 and 2000 (Frayer *et al.* 1983; Tiner 1984; Dahl and Johnson 1991; and Dahl 2000).

These wetland status and trend reports have been used by federal, state, local and tribal governments to develop wetland conservation strategies, measure the efficacy of existing policies, and validate comprehensive performance toward halting loss and regaining wetlands. Industry, the scientific community, conservation groups, decision makers and the public value this contemporary information for planning, decision-making, and on-the-ground management.

Our nation's wetlands goals have historically been based on wetland acreage and the ability to provide a quantitative measure of the extent of wetland area as a means to measure progress toward achieving the national goal of "no net loss." This concept was first formulated as a national goal by the National Wetlands Policy Forum (The Conservation Foundation 1988) and was later adopted as federal policy by President George H.W. Bush. In an effort to monitor the status and trends in the quantity and type of our nation's wetlands, a series of Fish and Wildlife Service reports have documented a steadily declining wetland loss rate. From the mid 1950s to the mid 1970s, the nation lost about 458,000 wetland acres annually. This rate of loss was substantially reduced to about 59,000 acres annually by 1997.

On Earth Day 2004, President George W. Bush announced a wetlands initiative that established a federal policy beyond "no net loss" of wetlands. The policy seeks to attain an overall increase in the quality and quantity of wetlands and set a goal of restoring, improving and protecting more than 3 million acres (1.2 million ha) in five years (Council on Environmental Quality 2005). To continue tracking wetland trends, the President further directed the Fish and Wildlife Service to complete an updated wetlands status and trends study in 2005—five years ahead of the mandated legislative schedule.

This updated report used the latest technologies in remote sensing, geospatial analysis and computerized mapping. The most recent aerial and satellite imagery available was analyzed to document wetland change on 4,682 two-mile square (5.2 sq. km) sample plots located throughout the 48 states. It covers the period from 1998 to 2004, and provides the most recent and comprehensive quantitative measure of the areal extent of all wetlands in the conterminous United States regardless of ownership. The study provides no qualitative assessments of wetland functions.

Figure 1. A cypress (Taxodium distichum) wetland near the White River, Arkansas, 2005.

Study Design and Procedures

Study Objectives

This study was designed to provide the nation with current, scientifically valid information on the status and extent of wetland resources regardless of ownership and to measure change in those resources over time.

Wetland Definition and Classification

The Fish and Wildlife Service used the Cowardin *et al.* (1979) definition of wetland. This definition is the standard for the agency and is the national standard for wetland mapping, monitoring and data reporting as determined by the Federal Geographic Data Committee. It is a two-part definition as indicated below:

Ephemeral waters, which are not recognized as a wetland type, and certain types of "farmed wetlands" as defined by the Food Security Act were not included in this study because they do not meet the Cowardin *et al.* definition. The definition and classification of wetland types have been consistent in every status and trends study conducted by the Fish and Wildlife Service. Habitat category definitions are given in synoptic form in Table 1. The reader is encouraged to also review Appendix A, which provides complete definitions of wetland types and land use categories used in this study.

Wetlands are lands transitional between terrestrial and aquatic systems where the water table is usually at or near the surface or the land is covered by shallow water.

For purposes of this classification wetlands must have one or more of the following three attributes: (1) at least periodically, the land supports predominantly hydrophytes, (2) the substrate is predominantly undrained hydric soil, and (3) the substrate is nonsoil and is saturated with water or covered by shallow water at some time during the growing season of each year.

Figure 2. A gallery of wetland images. From top to bottom left; emergent marsh in Wisconsin, black-crowned night heron (Nycticorax nycticorax) (FWS), shrub wetland in Michigan (courtesy of St. Mary's University), Bosque del Apache National Wildlife Refuge, New Mexico (FWS). From top to bottom right; forested wetland (FWS), Parker River National Wildlife Refuge, Massachusetts (FWS), freshwater wetland, northern Indiana, 2005, American toad (Bufo americanus) (Isaac Chellman, USGS).

Deepwater Habitats

Wetlands and deepwater habitats are defined separately by Cowardin *et al.* (1979) because the term wetland does not include deep, permanent water bodies. Deepwater habitats are permanently flooded land lying below the deepwater boundary of wetlands (Figure 3). Deepwater habitats include environments where surface water is permanent and often deep, so that water, rather than air, is the principal medium in which the dominant organisms live, whether or not they are attached to the substrate. For the purposes of conducting status and trends work, all lacustrine (lake) and riverine (river) waters were considered deepwater habitats.

Upland Habitats

An abbreviated upland classification system patterned after the U. S. Geological Survey land classification scheme described by Anderson *et al.* (1976), with five generalized categories, was used to describe uplands in this study. These categories are listed in Table 1.

Figure 3. Open water lakes, such as this reservoir were classified as deepwater habitats if they exceeded 20 acres (8 ha). Piney Run Lake, Maryland, 2005.

Table 1. Wetland, deepwater, and upland categories used to conduct wetland status and trends studies. The definitions for each category appear in Appendix A.

Category	Common Description
Salt Water Habitats	
Marine Subtidal*	Open ocean
Marine Intertidal	Near shore
Estuarine Subtidal*	Open-water/bay bottoms
Estuarine Intertidal Emergents	Salt marsh
Estuarine Intertidal Forested/Shrub	Mangroves or other estuarine shrubs
Estuarine Unconsolidated Shore	Beaches/bars
Estuarine Aquatic Bed	Submerged or floating estuarine vegetation
Riverine* (may be tidal or nontidal)	River systems
Freshwater Habitats	
Palustrine Forested	Forested swamps
Palustrine Shrub	Shrub wetlands
Palustrine Emergents	Inland marshes/wet meadows
Palustrine Unconsolidated Shore	Shore beaches/bars
Palustrine Unconsolidated Bottom	Open-water ponds
Palustrine Aquatic Bed	Floating aquatic/submerged vegetations
Palustrine Farmed	Farmed wetland
Lacustrine*	Lakes and reservoirs
Uplands	
Agriculture	Cropland, pasture, managed rangeland
Urban	Cities and incorporated developments
Forested Plantations	Planted or intensively managed forests, silviculture
Rural Development	Non-urban developed areas and infrastructure
Other Uplands (see further explanation in Appendix A)	Rural uplands not in any other category; barren lands

*Deepwater habitat

Sampling Design

This study measured wetland extent and change using a statistically stratified, simple random sampling design, the foundations of which are well documented (Dahl 2000; USFWS 2004b). The sampling design used for this study was developed by an interagency group of spatial sampling experts specifically to monitor wetland change. It can be used to monitor conversions between ecologically different wetland types, as well as measure wetland gains and losses.

Sample plots were examined, with the use of remotely sensed data in combination with field work, to determine wetland change. To monitor changes in wetland area, the 48 conterminous states were stratified or divided by state boundaries and 35 physiographical subdivisions described by Hammond (1970) (Appendix B).

Monitoring Wetlands

Stratification of the nation based on differences in wetland density makes this study an effective measure of wetland resources. Some natural resource assessments stop at county boundaries or at a point coinciding with the census line for inhabitable land area. Doing so may exclude offshore wetlands, shallow water embayments or sounds, shoals, sand bars, tidal flats and reefs (Figure 4). These are important fish and wildlife habitats.

The Fish and Wildlife Service included wetlands in coastal areas by adding a supplemental sampling stratum along the Atlantic and Gulf coastal fringes. This stratum includes the near shore areas of the coast with its barrier islands, coastal marshes, exposed tidal flats and other offshore features not a part of the landward physiographic zones. The coastal zone stratum, included 28.2 million acres (11.4 million ha). At its widest point in southern Louisiana, this zone extended about 92.6 miles (149 km) from Lake

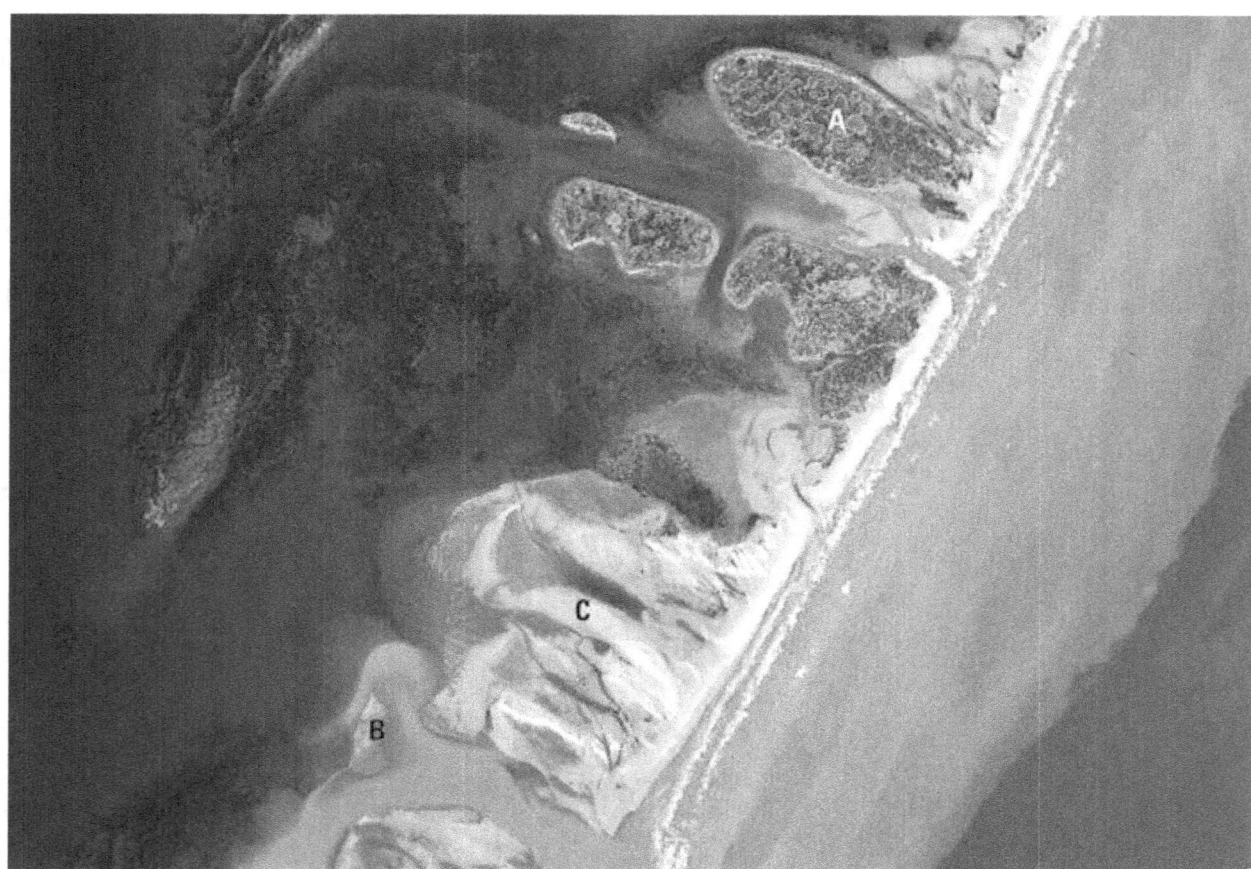

Figure 4. Coastal wetlands offshore from the mainland, include salt marsh (estuarine emergent) (A), shoals (B), tidal flats (C) and bars. National Aerial Photography Program, color infrared photograph, coastal Louisiana, 2004.

Pontchartrain to the furthest extent of estuarine wetland resources. In this area, saltwater was the overriding influence on biological systems. The coastal zone in this study was not synonymous with any state or federal jurisdictional coastal zone definitions. The legal definition of "coastal zone" has been developed for use in coastal demarcations, planning, regulatory and management activities undertaken by other federal or state agencies.

To permit even spatial coverage of the sample plots and to allow results to be computed easily by sets of states, the 36 physiographic regions formed by the Hammond subdivisions and the coastal zone stratum were intersected with state boundaries to form 220 subdivisions or strata. An example of this stratification approach and the way it relates to sampling frequency is shown for North Carolina (Figure 5).

In the physiographic strata described above, weighted, stratified sample plots were randomly allocated in proportion to the amount of wetland acreage expected to occur in each stratum. Each sample area was a surface plot 2.0 miles (3.2 km) on a side or 4.0 square miles of area equaling 2,560 acres (1,036 ha). The study included all wetlands regardless of land ownership.

This study re-analyzed the land area for 4,371 existing sample plots used for past wetlands status and trends studies. Three hundred eleven supplemental sample plots were added to Ohio, Indiana, Illinois, Iowa, Missouri, North Dakota, South Dakota, California, Oklahoma and Texas. Augmentation was done to provide more finite measurement and equitable spatial coverage of plots, since loss rates had been declining historically. This brought the total number of sample plots used in this study to 4,682.

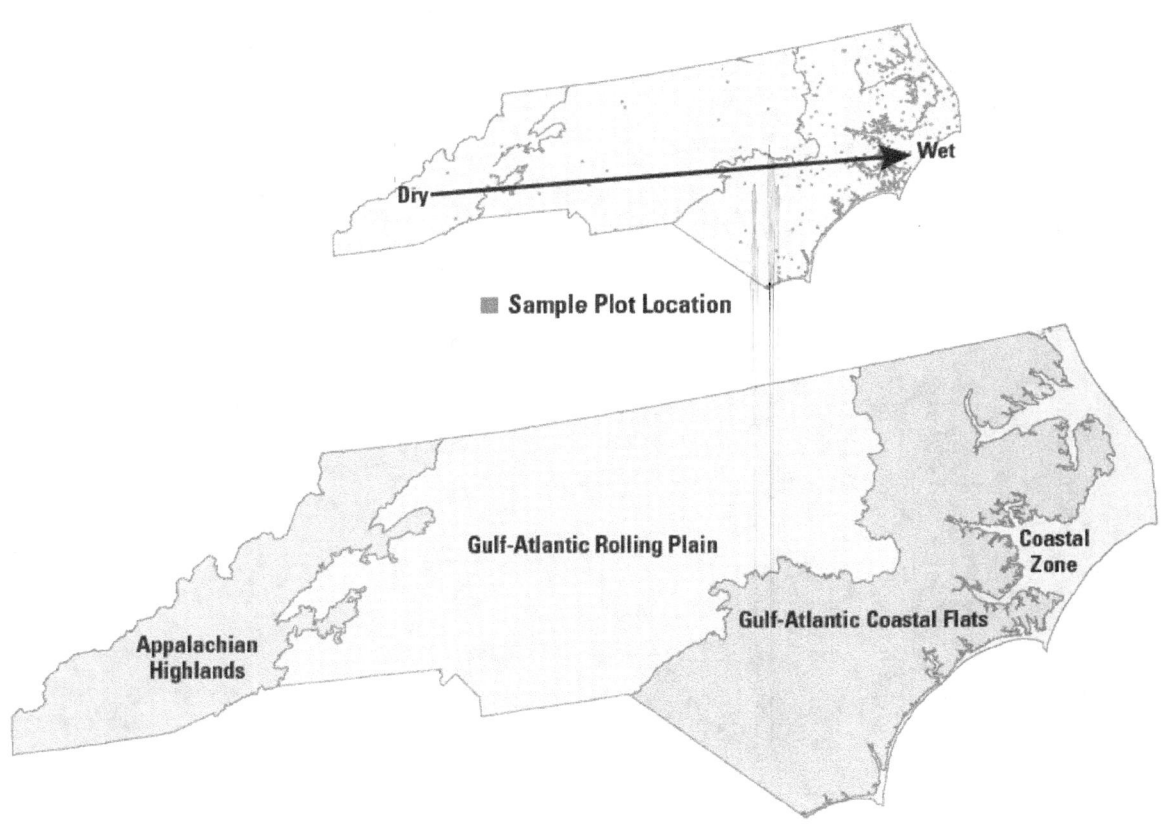

Figure 5. Physiographic subdivisions of North Carolina and sample plot distribution as used in this study.

Types and Dates of Imagery

Image analysts relied primarily on observable physical or spectral characteristics evident on high altitude imagery, in conjunction with collateral data, to make decisions regarding wetland classification and deepwater determinations[3].

---

[3]Analysis of imagery was supplemented with substantial field work and ground observations.

Remote sensing techniques to detect and monitor wetlands in the United States and Canada have been used successfully by a number academic researchers and governmental agencies (Dechka *et al.* 2002; Watmough *et al.* 2002; Tiner 1996; National Research Council 1995; Patience and Klemas 1993; Lillesand and Kiefer 1987; Aldrich 1979). The use of remotely sensed data, either from aircraft or satellite, is a cost effective way to conduct surveys over expansive areas (Dahl 1990a). The Fish and Wildlife Service has used remote sensing techniques to determine the biological extent of wetlands for the past 30 years. To monitor wetland change, only high quality imagery was acquired and used.

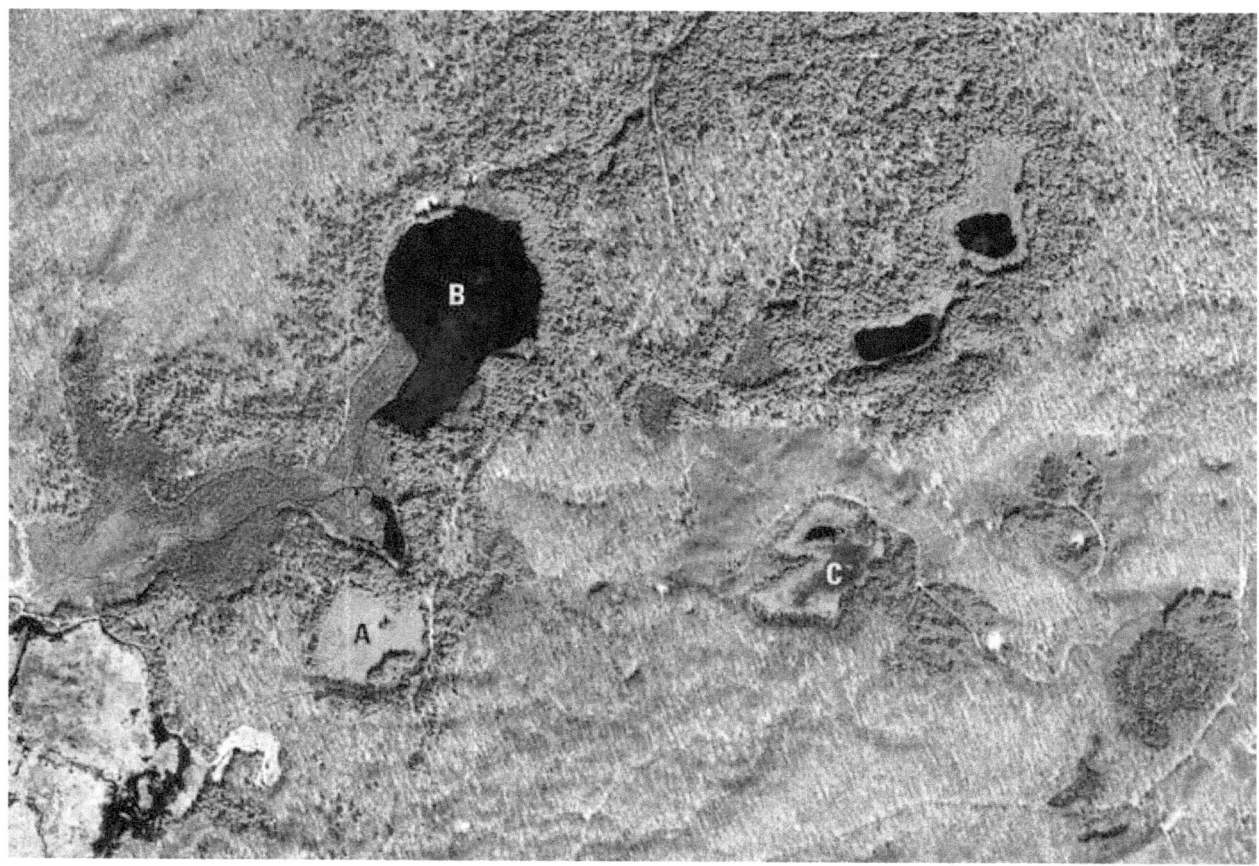

Figure 6. High resolution, infrared Ikonos satellite image of bogs (A), lakes (B) and wetlands (C) of northern Wisconsin, spring 2005. Image courtesy of Space Imaging Corp.

This study used multiple sources of recent imagery and direct on-the-ground observations to record wetland changes. To recognize and classify wetland vegetation, color infrared imagery was preferred (Figure 6). Experienced wetland interpreters have found color infrared to be superior to other imagery types for recognition and classification of wetland vegetation types (USFWS 2004b).

Wherever possible, leaf-off (early spring or late fall) imagery was used. Imagery obtained when vegetation was dormant allowed for better identification of wetland boundaries, areas covered by water, drainage patterns, separation of coniferous from deciduous forest, and classification of some understory vegetation (Tiner 1996). There are distinct advantages to using leaf-off imagery to detect the extent of

forested wetlands. Leaf off imagery enhances the visual evidence of hydrologic conditions such as saturation, flooding, or ponding (Figure 7). This imagery, combined with collateral data including soil surveys, topographic maps, and wetland maps were used to identify and delineate the areal extent of wetlands.

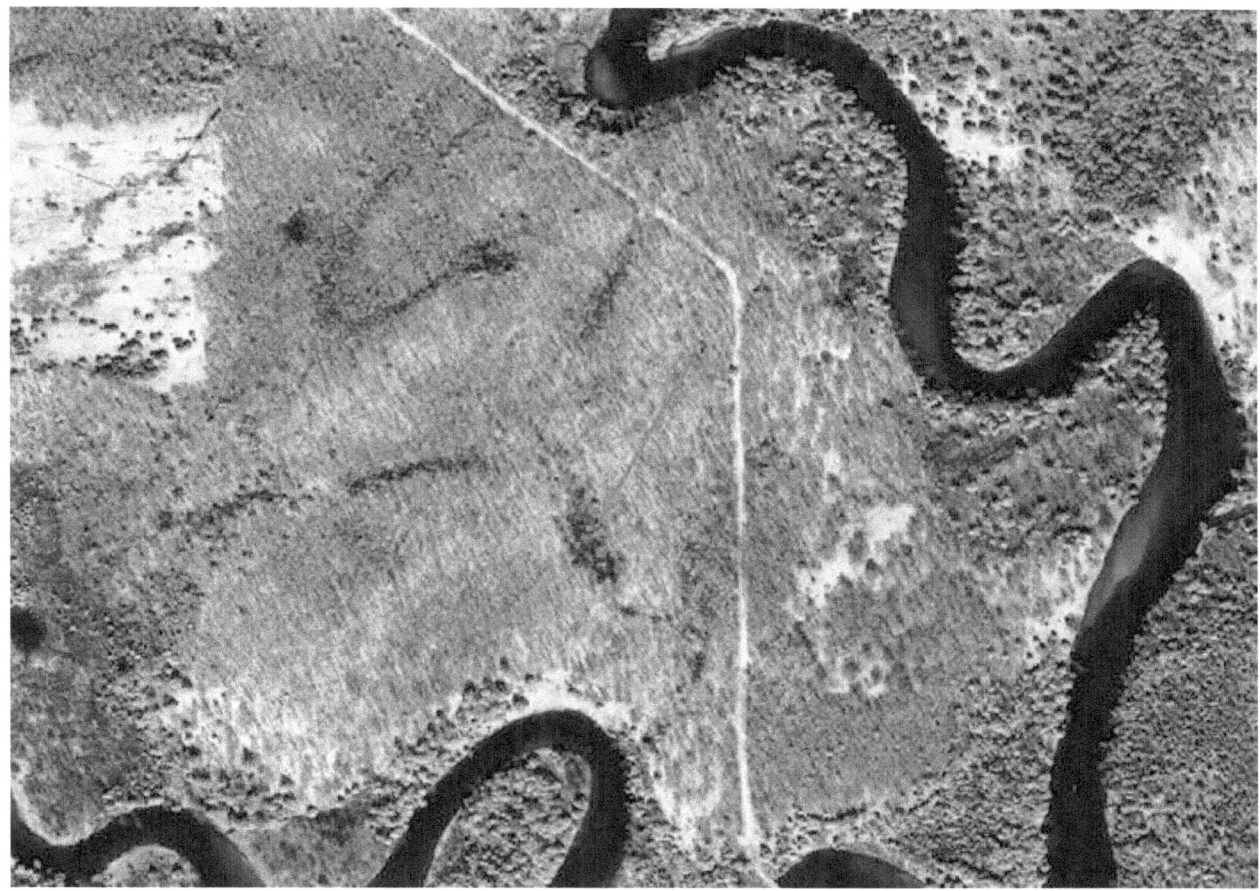

Figure 7. Early spring 2005 Ikonos satellite image of Michigan. Leaf-off condition made recognition of wetland features easier. These old oxbows or swales (indicated by red arrows) can be masked by heavy tree canopy later in the growing season. Image courtesy of Space Imaging Corp.

In 2004, recent aerial photographic coverage for large portions of the country was not available. Multiple sources of satellite imagery in combination with recently acquired digital photography were used to complete this study. Satellite imagery made up about 45 percent of the source material used for this analysis. Advantages included higher resolution digital imagery that was acquired close to the target reporting date. The mean dates of the imagery used, by state, are shown in Figure 8.

Satellite imagery was supplemented with National Agriculture Imagery Program (NAIP) imagery acquired during the agricultural growing season (Figure 9). NAIP imagery made up about 30 percent of the source imagery. (For technical specifications of NAIP imagery see www.apfo.usda.gov/NAIP/ .) The remaining imagery needed to complete the study was acquired through various sources of high resolution aerial photography.

Figure 8. Mean date of imagery used by state.

Figure 9. True color NAIP photographs show farmland (A), forest (B) and wetlands (C) above, and newly-created ponds in a housing development (D) at right. Indiana, 2003.

Technological Advances

Technological advances in the quality of remotely sensed imagery, computerized mapping techniques, and modernization of data management systems enhanced the ability to capture more detailed and timely information about the nation's wetlands. The use of these technologies greatly improved the administration, access, management and integration of the spatial data. Such advances required modernization of procedural techniques for image interpretation, data capture and operational management. Some of the data modernization process involved development of customized software tools to execute tasks specific to wetland attribution, provide logic checking functions and verification of the digital status and trends data. These procedural updates were incorporated into a revised technical procedures and protocols manual (USFWS 2004b).

Methods of Data Collection and Image Analysis

The delineation of wetlands through image analysis forms the foundation for deriving all subsequent products and results. Consequently, a great deal of emphasis has been placed on the quality of the image interpretation. The Fish and Wildlife Service makes no attempt to adapt or apply the products of these techniques to regulatory or legal authorities regarding wetland boundary determinations or to jurisdiction or land ownership, but rather the information was used to assist in making trend estimates characterizing wetland habitats.

General information on photo interpretation techniques is provided by various authors (Avery 1968; Lillesand and Kiefer 1987; Philipson 1996). Specific protocols used for image interpretation of wetlands are documented in the Status and Trends technical manual (USFWS 2004b).

Wetlands were identified based on vegetation, visible hydrology and geography. Delineations on the sample plots reflected ecological change or changes in land use that influenced the size, distribution or classification of wetland habitats.

The minimum targeted delineation unit for wetland was one acre (0.40 ha). The actual smallest size of wetland features delineated was about 0.005 acres (0.002 ha). However, not all features this size, or smaller, were detected (Figure 10).

Figure 10. A small wetland basin estimated to have been about seven square meters. Some wetlands this size were detectable using high resolution imagery.

Wetland Change Detection

Remotely sensed imagery was the primary data for wetland change detection. It was used in conjunction with reliable collateral data such as topographic maps, coastal navigation charts, soils information, and historical imagery or studies. Field verification also played an important role and was used to address questions regarding image interpretation, land use classification and attribution of wetland gains or losses.

For each sample plot, the extent of change among all wetland types between the two dates of imagery was used to estimate the total area of each wetland type (Figure 11) and the changes in wetland area and type between the two dates. The changes were recorded in categories that can be considered the result of either natural change, such as the natural succession of emergent wetlands to shrub wetlands, or human induced change. Areas of sample plots that were identified in the initial era as wetland but are no longer wetland were placed into five land use categories (agriculture, upland forested plantations, upland areas of rural development, upland urban landscapes and other miscellaneous lands) based upon the land use evident on the most recent imagery. The outputs from this analysis were change matrices that provided estimates of wetland area by type and observed changes over time. Rigorous quality control inspections were built into the interpretation, data collection and analysis processes.

Difficulties in determining wetland change can be related to timing or quality of the imagery (Dahl 2004). Imagery acquired at the time of abnormal hydrologic conditions, such as flooding or drought, can make determination of wetland change challenging. In these instances field work was required to assist image analysts in making appropriate wetlands determinations.

Misinterpretation of wetland loss or gain could result from factors such as farming of wetlands during dry cycles, drought conditions, excess

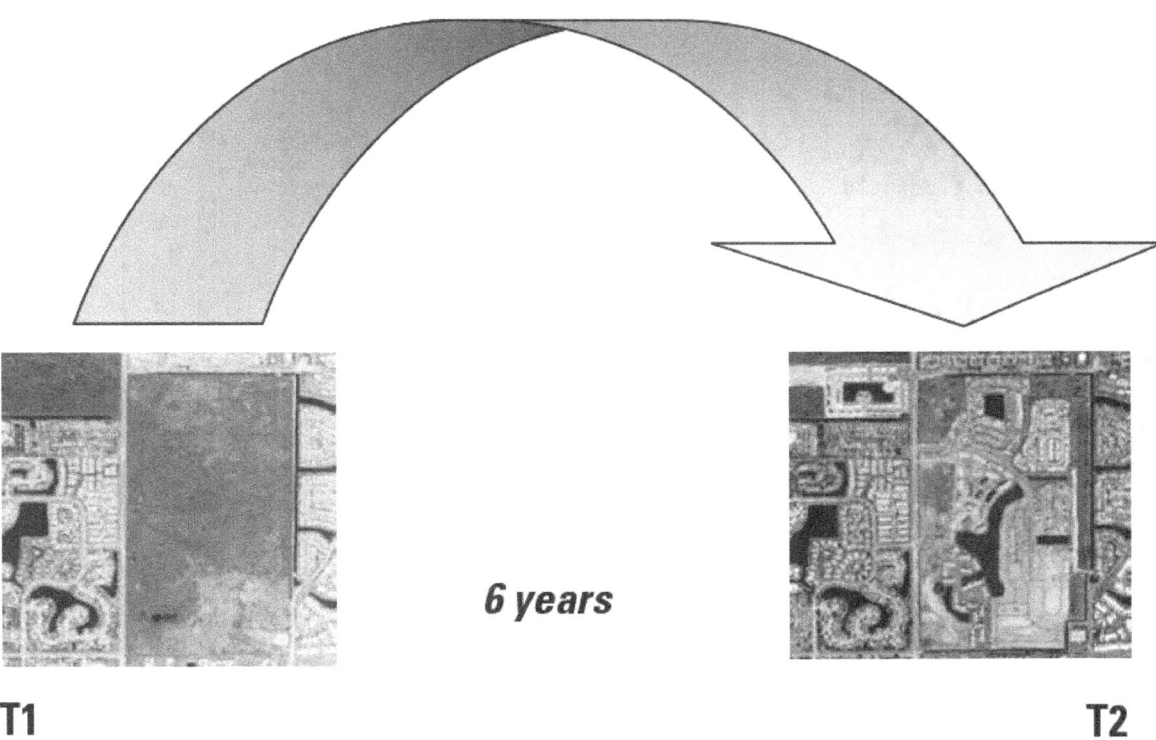

6 years

T1

T2

Figure 11. Change detection involved a comparison of plots at two different times (T1 and T2).

surface water or flooding. False changes were avoided by observing visual evidence of a change in land management practices. This included the presence of new drainage ditches (Figure 12), canals or other man-made water courses, evidence of dredging, spoil deposition or fills, impoundments or excavations, structures, pavement or hardened surfaces, in addition to the lack of any hydrology, vegetation or soil indicators indicative of wetland.

Some land use practices can also affect wetland change detection. Disturbed sites often had ambiguous remotes sensing indicators. Disturbed areas were indicative of lands in transition from one land use to another (Figure 13). Upon field inspection, these areas often had altered hydrology, soils or vegetation making wetland classification and change determination more difficult. In these instances, field inspection of the wetland site and surrounding area provided additional information.

Figure 12. A true color aerial photograph shows a new drainage network (indicated by red arrow) and provides visual evidence of wetland loss. Lack of wetland vegetation, surface water or soil saturation further indicates that this wetland had been effectively drained.

Figure 13. Lands in transition from one land use category to another pose unique challenges for image analysts. Field inspection of this site indicated the area was under construction as part of a highway project.

Field Verification

Field verification was completed for 1,504 (32 percent) of the sample plots distributed in 35 States (Figure 14). This constituted the largest field verification effort undertaken for a status and trends report. Field work was done primarily as a quality control measure to verify that plot delineations were correct. Verification involved field visits to a cross section of wetland types and geographic settings, and to plots with different image types, scales and dates. Field work was not done in some western states because of the remote location (limited access) of sample plots. Of the 1,504 sample plots reviewed in the field, 720 used satellite imagery and 784 used high altitude aerial photography. All field verification work took place between March and September, 2005[4]. Representatives from four states and seven federal agencies participated in field reconnaissance trips. In rare instances, field work was used to update sample plots based on observations of on-the-ground conditions.

---

[4] Results of field verification work indicated no discernable differences in the size or classification of wetlands delineated using either satellite imagery or the high altitude photography. Errors of wetland omission were two percent based on occurrence but less than one percent based on area (omitted wetlands were generally small < 1.0 acre or 2.47 ha). Errors of inclusion of upland were less than one percent in both occurrence and area. There was no difference regionally, between states or data analysts in the number of errors found based on field inspections, although not all plots were included in the field analysis.

States not field verified
States field verified

Figure 14. Field verification was completed at sites in 35 states shown on the map.

Quality Control

To ensure the reliability of wetland status and trends data, the Fish and Wildlife Service adhered to established quality assurance and quality control measures for data collection, analysis, verification and reporting. Some of the major quality control steps included:

Plot Location and Positional Accuracy

Status and trends sample plots were permanently fixed georeferenced areas used to monitor land use and cover type changes. The same plot population has been re-analyzed for each status and trends report cycle. The plot coordinates were positioned precisely using a system of redundant backup locators on prints produced from a geographic information system, topographic maps (Figure 15), other maps used for collateral information and the aerial imagery. Plot outlines were computer generated for the correct spatial coordinates, size and projection (Figure 16).

Quality Control of Interpreted Images

This study used well established, time-tested, fully documented data collection conventions (USFWS 1994a; 1994b; 2004b). It employed a small cadre of highly skilled and experienced personnel for image interpretation and processing.

All interpreted imagery was reviewed by a technical expert in ecological change detection. The reviewing analyst adhered to all standards, quality requirements and technical specifications and reviewed 100 percent of the work.

Data Verification

All digital data files were subjected to rigorous quality control inspections. Digital data verification included quality control checks that addressed the geospatial correctness, digital integrity and some cartographic aspects of the data. These steps took place following the review and qualitative acceptance of the ecological data. Implementation of quality checks ensured that the data conformed to the specified criteria, thus achieving the project objectives.

Quality Assurance of Digital Data Files

There were tremendous advantages in using newer technologies to store and analyze the geographic data. The geospatial analysis capability built into this study provided a complete digital database to better assist analysis of wetland change information.

All digital data files were subjected to rigorous quality control inspections. Automated checking modules incorporated in the geographic information system (Arc/GIS) were used to correct digital artifacts including polygon topology. Additional customized data inspections were made to ensure that the changes indicated at the image interpretation stage were properly executed. Digital file quality control reviews also provided confirmation of plot location, stratum assignment, and total land or water area sampled.

A customized digital data verification software package designed specifically for status and trends work was used. It checked for improbable changes that may represent errors in the image interpretation. The software considered the length of time between update cycles, identified certain unrealistic cover-type changes such open water ponds changing to forested wetland, and other types of potential errors in the digital data.

Figure 15. Topographic maps in digital raster graphics format were used as auxilliary information and for quality control.

Figure 16. Digital wetlands status and trends data were viewed combined with contemporary georeferenced color infrared imagery of the study areas.

Statistical Analysis

The wetland status and trends study was based on a scientific probability sample of the surface area of the 48 conterminous States. The area sampled was about 1.93 billion acres (0.8 billion ha), and the sampling did not discriminate based on land ownership. The study used a stratified, simple random sampling design. About 754,000 possible sample plots comprised the total population. Given this population, the sampling design was stratified by use of the 36 physical subdivisions described in the "Study Design" section. This stratification scheme had ecological, statistical, and practical advantages. The study design was well suited for determining wetland acreage trends because the 36 divisions of the United States coincide with factors that effect wetland distribution and abundance. Once stratified, the land subdivisions represented large areas where the samples were distributed to obtain an even spatial representation of plots. The final stratification, based on intersecting physiographic land types with state boundaries, guaranteed an improved spatial random sample of plots.

Geographic information system software organized the information about the 4,682 random sample plots. An important design feature crucial to understanding the technical aspects of this study is that a grid of full-sized square plots can be overlaid on any stratum to define the population of sampling units for that stratum. However, at the stratum boundaries some plots were "split" across the boundary and thus, were not a full 2,560 acres (1,036 ha). In sampling theory, plot size is an auxiliary variable that is known for all sampled plots and whose total is known over every stratum. All sampling units (plots) in a stratum were given equal selection probabilities regardless of their size. In the data analysis phase, the adjustments were made for varying plot sizes by use of ratio estimation theory. For any wetland type, the proportion of its area in the sample of plots in a stratum was an unbiased estimator of the unknown proportion of that type in that stratum. Inference about total wetland acreage by wetland type or for all wetlands in any stratum began with the ratio (r) of the relevant total acreage observed in the sample (T_y), for that stratum divided by the total area of the sample (T_x). Thus, y was measured in each sample plot; $r = T_y/T_x$, and the estimated total acreage of the relevant wetland type in the stratum was A x r. The sum of these estimated totals over all strata provided the national estimate for the wetland type in question. Uncertainty, which was measured as sampling variance of an estimate, was estimated based on the variation among the sample proportions in a stratum (the estimation of sample variation is highly technical and not presented here). The sampling variation of the national total was the sum of the sampling variance over all strata. These methods are standard for ratio estimation in association with a stratified random sampling design (Sarndal *et al.* 1992; Thompson 1992).

By use of this statistical procedure, the sample plot data were expanded to specific physiographic regions, by wetland type, and statistical estimates were generated for the 48 conterminous States. The reliability of each estimate generated is expressed as the percent coefficient of variation (% C.V.) associated with that estimate. Percent coefficient of variation was expressed as (standard deviation/mean) x (100). The percent coefficient of variation indicates that there was a 95 percent probability that an estimate was within the indicated percentage range of the true value.

Procedural Error

Procedural or measurement errors occur in the data collection phase of any study and must be considered. Procedural error is related to the ability to accurately recognize and classify wetlands both from multiple sources of imagery and on-the-ground evaluations. Types of procedural errors may have included missed wetlands, inclusion of upland as wetland, misclassification of wetlands or misinterpretation of data collection protocols. The amount of introduced procedural error is usually a function of the quality of the data collection conventions; the number, variability, training and experience of data collection personnel; and the rigor of any quality control or quality assurance measures.

Rigorous quality control reviews and redundant inspections were incorporated into the data collection and data entry processes to help reduce the level of procedural error. Estimated procedural error ranged from 3 to 5 percent of the true values when all quality assurance measures had been completed.

Limitations

The identification of wetland habitats through image analysis forms the basis for wetland status and trends data results. Because of the limitations of aerial imagery as the primary data source to detect some wetlands, the Fish and Wildlife Service excludes certain wetland types from its monitoring efforts.

These limitations included the inability to detect small areas; inability to accurately map or monitor certain types of wetlands such as sea grasses (Orth *et al.* 1990), submerged aquatic vegetation, or submerged reefs (Dahl 2005); and inability to consistently identify certain forested wetlands (Tiner 1990).

Other habitats intentionally excluded from this study include:

Estuarine wetlands of the Pacific coast—Unlike the broad expanses of emergent wetlands along the Gulf and Atlantic coasts, the estuarine wetlands of California, Oregon and Washington occur in discontinuous patches (Figure 17). Their patchy distribution precludes establishment of a coastal stratum similar to that of the Gulf and Atlantic coast wetlands and no statistically valid data could be obtained through establishment of a Pacific coastal stratum. Therefore, consistent with past studies, this study did not sample Pacific coast estuarine wetlands such as those in San Francisco Bay, California; Coos Bay, Oregon; or Puget Sound, Washington.

Figure 17. The Pacific coastline, Three Arch Rocks National Wildlife Refuge, Oregon. Photo courtesy of FWS.

Commercial Rice—Throughout the southeastern United States and in California, rice (*Oryza sativa*) is planted on drained hydric soils and on upland soils. When rice was being grown, the land was flooded and the area functioned as wetland (Figures 18A and B). In years when rice was not grown, the same fields were used to grow other crops (e.g., corn, soybeans, cotton). Commercial rice lands were identified primarily in California, Arkansas, Louisiana, Mississippi and Texas. These cultivated rice fields were not able to support hydrophytic vegetation. Consequently, the Fish and Wildlife Service did not include these lands in the base wetland acreage estimates.

Figures 18A and B. Commercial rice fields where water was pumped to flood the rice crop. These fields were drained when they were in upland crop rotation. Central Arkansas, 2005.

Attribution of Wetland Losses

The process of identifying or attributing cause for wetland losses or gains has been investigated by both the Fish and Wildlife Service and Natural Resources Conservation Service. In 1998 and 1999, the Natural Resources Conservation Service and the Fish and Wildlife Service made a concerted effort to develop a uniform approach to attribute wetland losses and gains to their causes. The categories used to determine the causes of wetland losses and gains are described below.

Agriculture

The definition of agriculture followed Anderson *et al.* (1976) and included land used primarily for production of food and fiber.

Agricultural activity was shown by distinctive geometric field and road patterns on the landscape and/or by tracks produced by livestock or mechanized equipment. Agricultural land uses included horticultural crops, row and close grown crops, hayland, pastureland, native pastures and range land and farm infrastructures (Figure 19A and B). Examples of agricultural activities in each land use include:

Horticultural crops consisted of orchard fruits (limes, grapefruit, oranges, other citrus, apples, peaches and like species). Also included were nuts such as almonds, pecans and walnuts; vineyards including grapes and hops; bush-fruit such as blueberries; berries such as strawberries or raspberries; and commercial flower and fern growing operations.

Row and Close Grown Crops included field corn, sugar cane, sweet corn, sorghum, soybeans, cotton, peanuts, tobacco, sugar beets, potatoes, and truck crops such as melons, beets, cauliflower, pumpkins, tomatoes, sunflower and watermelon. Close grown crops also included wheat, oats, barley, sod, ryegrass, and similar graminoids.

Hayland and pastureland included grass, legumes, summer fallow and grazed native grassland.

Other farmland included farmsteads and ranch headquarters, commercial feedlots, greenhouses, hog facilities, nurseries and poultry facilities.

Figure 19A and B. Examples of agricultural land use include both this rangeland in western Nebraska, 2005 (A), and row crops such as this cornfield in the midwest, 2004 (B).

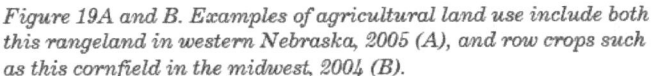

Forested Plantations

Forested plantations consisted of planted and managed forest stands and included planted pines, Christmas tree farms, clear cuts and other managed forest stands. These were identified by the following remote sensing indicators: 1) trees planted in rows or blocks; 2) forested blocks growing with uniform crown heights; or 3) logging activity and use patterns (Figure 20).

Rural Development

Rural developments occurred in rural and suburban settings outside distinct cities and towns. They were characterized by non intensive land use and sparse building density. Typically, a rural development was a crossroads community that had a corner gas station and a convenience store and was surrounded by sparse residential housing. Scattered suburban communities located outside of a major urban centers were also included in this category as were some industrial and commercial complexes; isolated transportation, power, and communication facilities; strip mines; quarries; and recreational areas such as golf courses. Major highways through rural development areas were included in the rural development category.

Figure 20. Trees planted in rows with uniform crown height (A) and block clear cuts [blue-green feature in center (B) were indicators of managed forest plantations. Color infrared Ikonos satellite image, Virginia 2004. Courtesy of Space Imaging Corp.

Urban Development

Urban land consisted of areas of intensive use in which much of the land was covered by structures (high building density as shown in Figure 21). Urbanized areas were cities and towns that provided goods and services through a central business district. Services such as banking, medical and legal office buildings, supermarkets and department stores made up the business center of a city. Commercial strip developments along main transportation routes, shopping centers, contiguous dense residential areas, industrial and commercial complexes, transportation, power and communication facilities, city parks, ball fields and golf courses were included in the urban category.

Other Land Uses

Other Land Use was composed of uplands not characterized by the previous categories. Typically these lands included native prairie, unmanaged or non patterned upland forests, conservation lands, scrub lands, and barren land. Lands in transition between different uses were also in this category.

Transitional lands were lands in transition from one land use to another. They generally occurred in large acreage blocks of 40 acres (16 ha) or more. They were characterized by the lack of any remote sensor information that would enable the interpreter to reliably predict future use. The transitional phase occurred when wetlands were drained, ditched, filled or when the vegetation had been removed and the area was temporarily bare.

Interagency field evaluations were conducted to test these definitions on the wetland status and trends plots to attribute wetland losses or gains. Field evaluation of these plots resulted in no disagreement among agency representatives with how the Fish and Wildlife Service attributed wetland losses or gains as to cause.

Figure 21. Urban wetlands (shown as dark blue-black) outside of a shopping mall are surrounded by high density urban development. New Jersey, 2003, color infrared photograph.

A freshwater wetland, Reelfoot Lake, Tennessee, 2005.

Results and Discussion

Status of the Nation's Wetlands

There were an estimated 107.7 million acres (43.6 million ha) of wetlands in the conterminous United States in 2004[5]. (The coefficient of variation of the national estimate was 2.7 percent.[6]) Wetlands composed 5.5 percent of the surface area of the conterminous United States (Figure 22). An estimated 95 percent of all wetlands were freshwater and five percent were in estuarine or marine systems. This overall distribution of wetlands by area and type had not changed from the previous era.

Data for the 1998 to 2004 study period are presented in a change matrix and shown in Appendix C. For ease of use, those data have been summarized and presented in Table 2.

Within the estuarine system, estuarine emergent (salt marsh—Figure 23) dominated, making up an estimated 73 percent (almost 3.9 million acres or 1.6 million ha) of all estuarine and marine wetlands. Estuarine shrub wetlands made up 13 percent of the area and non-vegetated saltwater wetlands 14 percent (Figure 24).

Among freshwater wetlands (Figure 25), freshwater forested wetlands made up the single largest category (51 percent). Freshwater emergent wetland made up an estimated 25.5 percent of the total area, shrub wetlands 17 percent and freshwater ponds 6.5 percent.

---

[5] This estimate reflects a 2.0 percent adjustment to the national wetland acreage base. This adjustment is within the 3 percent coefficient of variation associated with this estimation.
[6] 95 percent confidence interval

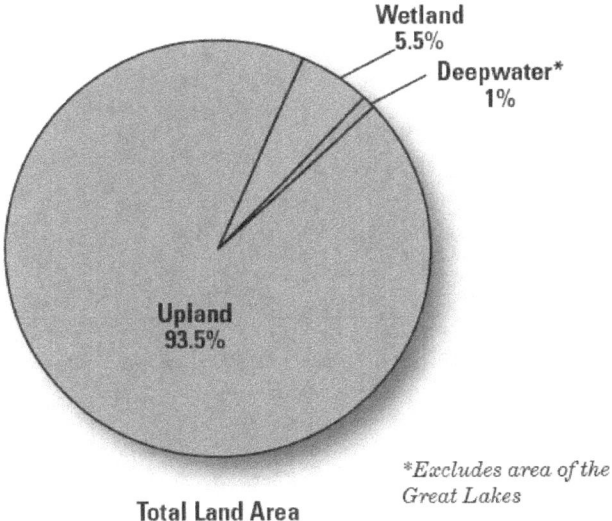

*Excludes area of the Great Lakes

Total Land Area

Figure 22. Wetland area compared to the total land area of the conterminous United States, 2004.

Table 2. Change in wetland area for selected wetland and deepwater categories, 1998 to 2004. The coefficient of variation (CV) for each entry (expressed as a percentage) is given in parentheses.

Wetland/Deepwater Category	Area, In Thousands of Acres			
	Estimated Area, 1998	Estimated Area, 2004	Change, 1998–2004	Change (In Percent)
Marine	130.4 (20.2)	128.6 (20.5)	—1/9 (68.7)	–1.4
Estuarine Intertidal Non-Vegetated[1]	594.1 (10.7)	600.0 (10.3)	5.9 *	1.0
Estuarine Intertidal Vegetated[2]	4,604.2 (4.0)	4,571.7 (4.0)	–32.4 (32.7)	–0.7
All Intertidal Wetlands	5,328.7 (3.8)	5,300.3 (3.8)	–28.4 (48.6)	–0.5
Freshwater Non-Vegetated[3]	5,918.7 (3.7)	6,633.9 (3.5)	715.3 (12.8)	12.1
Freshwater Ponds[4]	5,534.3 (3.7)	6,229.6 (3.5)	695.4 (13.1)	12.6
Freshwater Vegetated[5]	96,414.9 (3.0)	95,819.8 (3.0)	–495.1 (35.0)	–0.5
Freshwater Emergent	26,289.6 (8.0)	26,147.0 (8.0)	–142.6 *	–0.5
Freshwater Forested	51,483.1 (2.8)	52,031.4 (2.8)	548.2 (56.1)	1.1
Freshwater Shrub	18,542.2 (4.1)	17,641.4 (4.3)	–900.8 (34.2)	–4.9
All Freshwater Wetlands	102,233.6 (2.9)	102,453.8 (2.8)	220.2 (77.3)	0.2
All Wetlands	107,562.3 (2.7)	107,754.0 (2.7)	191.8 (89.1)	0.2
Deepwater Habitats				
Lacustrine[5]	16,610.5 (10.4)	16,773.4 (10.2)	162.9 (76.2)	1.0
Riverine	6,765.5 (9.1)	6,813.3 (9.1)	47.7 (68.8)	0.7
Estuarine Subtitdal	17.680.5 (2.2)	17.717.8 (2.2)	37.3 (40.8)	0.2
All Deepwater Habitats	41,046.6 (4.6)	41,304.5 (4.5)	247.9 (51.7)	0.6
All Wetlands and Deepwater Habitats[1,2]	148,618.8 (2.4)	149,058.5 (2.4)	439.7 (31.3)	0.3

*Statistically unreliable.

[1] Includes the categories: Estuarine Intertidal Aquatic Bed and Estuarine Intertidal Unconsolidated Shore.

[2] Includes the categories: Estuarine Intertidal Emergent and Estuarine Intertidal Shrub.

[3] Includes the categories: Palustrine Aquatic Bed, Palustrine Unconsolidated Bottom and Palustrine Unconsolidated Shore.

[4] Includes the categories: Palustrine Aquatic Bed, Palustrine Unconsolidated Bottom.

[5] Includes the categories: Palustrine Emergent, Palustrine Forested and Palustrine Shrub.

[6] Does non include the open-water area of the Great Lakes.

Percent coefficient of variation was expressed as (standard deviation/mean) x 100.

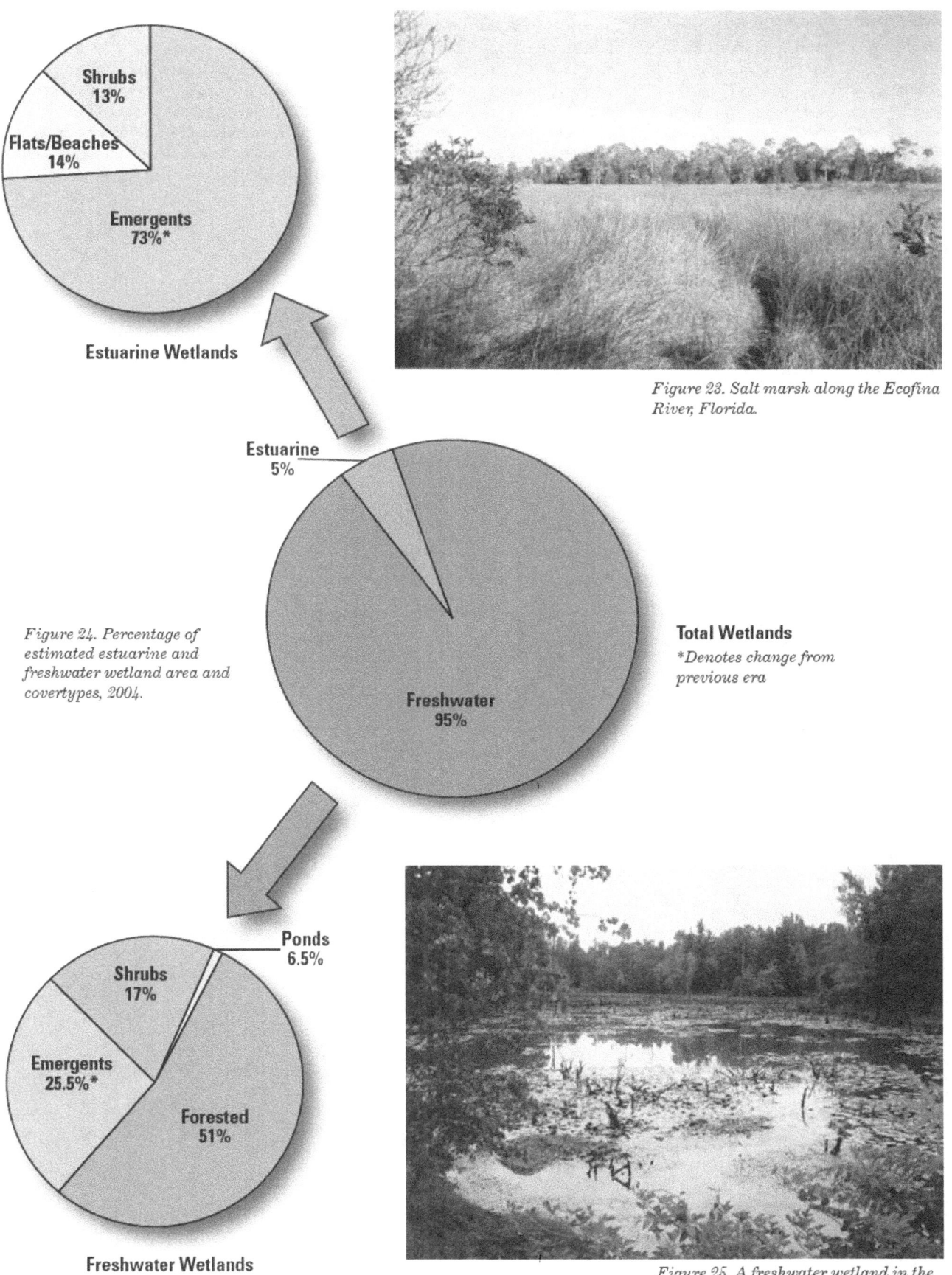

Shrubs
13%

Flats/Beaches
14%

Emergents
73%*

Estuarine Wetlands

Figure 23. Salt marsh along the Ecofina River, Florida.

Estuarine
5%

Figure 24. Percentage of estimated estuarine and freshwater wetland area and covertypes, 2004.

Total Wetlands
*Denotes change from previous era

Freshwater
95%

Ponds
6.5%

Shrubs
17%

Emergents
25.5%*

Forested
51%

Freshwater Wetlands

Figure 25. A freshwater wetland in the southeastern United States, 2005.

National Trends, 1998 to 2004

Between 1998 and 2004 there was an estimated net gain (Table 3) in wetlands of 191,750 acres (77,630 ha).[7] This equated to an average annual net gain of about 32,000 acres (12,900 ha) as seen in Figure 26. These estimates have led to the conclusion that wetland area gains achieved through restoration and creation have outdistanced losses. These data indicate a net gain in acreage but this report does not draw conclusions regarding trends in quality of the nation's wetlands

[7] There are statistical uncertainties associated with this estimate. The coefficient of variation expressed as a percentage is 89.1 percent for the net gain estimate.

Intertidal wetlands declined by an estimated 28,416 ac (11,500 ha) from 1998 to 2004. This was an average annual loss of about 4,740 acres (1,920 ha). The majority of these losses (94 percent) were to deepwater bay bottoms or open ocean.

Almost all net gains of wetland observed between 1998 and 2004 were in freshwater wetland types. The estimated net gain in freshwater wetland area between 1998 and 2004 was 220,200 acres (89,140 ha) as

seen in Table 2. Forested wetlands experienced a net gain. This can be explained by the maturation of wetland shrubs to forested wetlands. There was also a substantial increase in the number of open water ponds. Pond area increased by an estimated 12.6 percent over this study period.

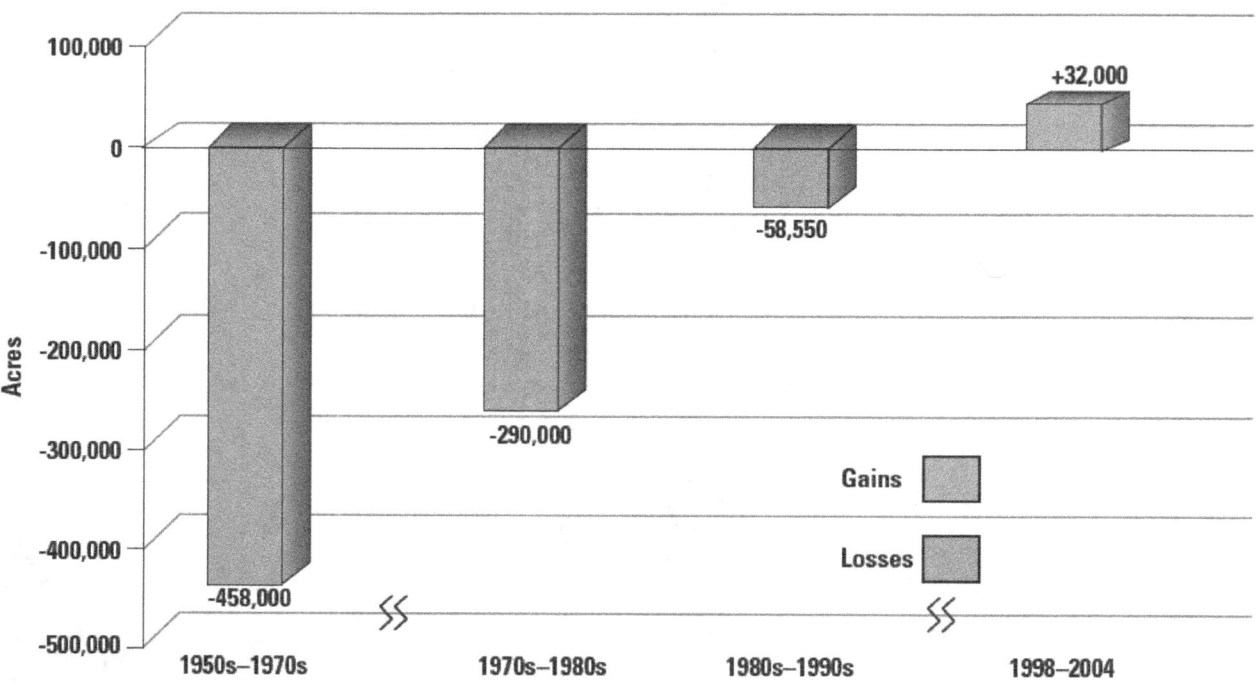

Figure 26. Average annual net loss and gain estimates for the conterminous United States, 1954 to 2004. Sources: Frayer et al. 1983; Dahl and Johnson 1991; Dahl 2000; and this study.

Attribution of Wetland Gain and Loss

Figure 27 depicts the categories that contributed wetland gains and those responsible for wetland losses over the course of this study. A net gain in wetland area was attributed to conversion of agricultural lands or former agricultural lands that had been idled in combination with wetland restorations from conservation lands in the "other" land use category.

Some freshwater wetland losses attributed to urban, rural development and silviculture offset some of the gains. An estimated 88,960 acres (36,000 ha) or 39 percent of the wetland losses, were lost to urban developments, 51,440 acres (20,800 ha), 22 percent were lost to rural development and 18,000 acres (7,300 ha), 8 percent of wetlands were lost through drainage or filling for silviculture. These losses were all the result of actions that destroyed the wetland hydrology. An additional 70,100 acres (28,400 ha), or 31 percent of the wetland area lost between 1998 and 2004 became deepwater habitats.

There were net gains from the "other" lands category and from Agriculture as a result of wetland restoration and conservation programs. An estimated 70,700 wetland acres (28,600 ha) came from agricultural lands and 349,600 acres (141,500 ha) from "other" uplands. These gains represented 17 percent of the net wetland gains from Agriculture and 83 percent from "other" uplands. Since the "other" uplands category includes lands in transition some of these wetlands may be subject to loss over time. Representative wetland restoration programs are listed in Appendix D.

Using the study definitions for the causes of wetland losses and gains, it was determined that urban development and rural development accounted for an estimated 140,400 acres (56,840 ha) or 61 percent of wetland loss over the course of this study.

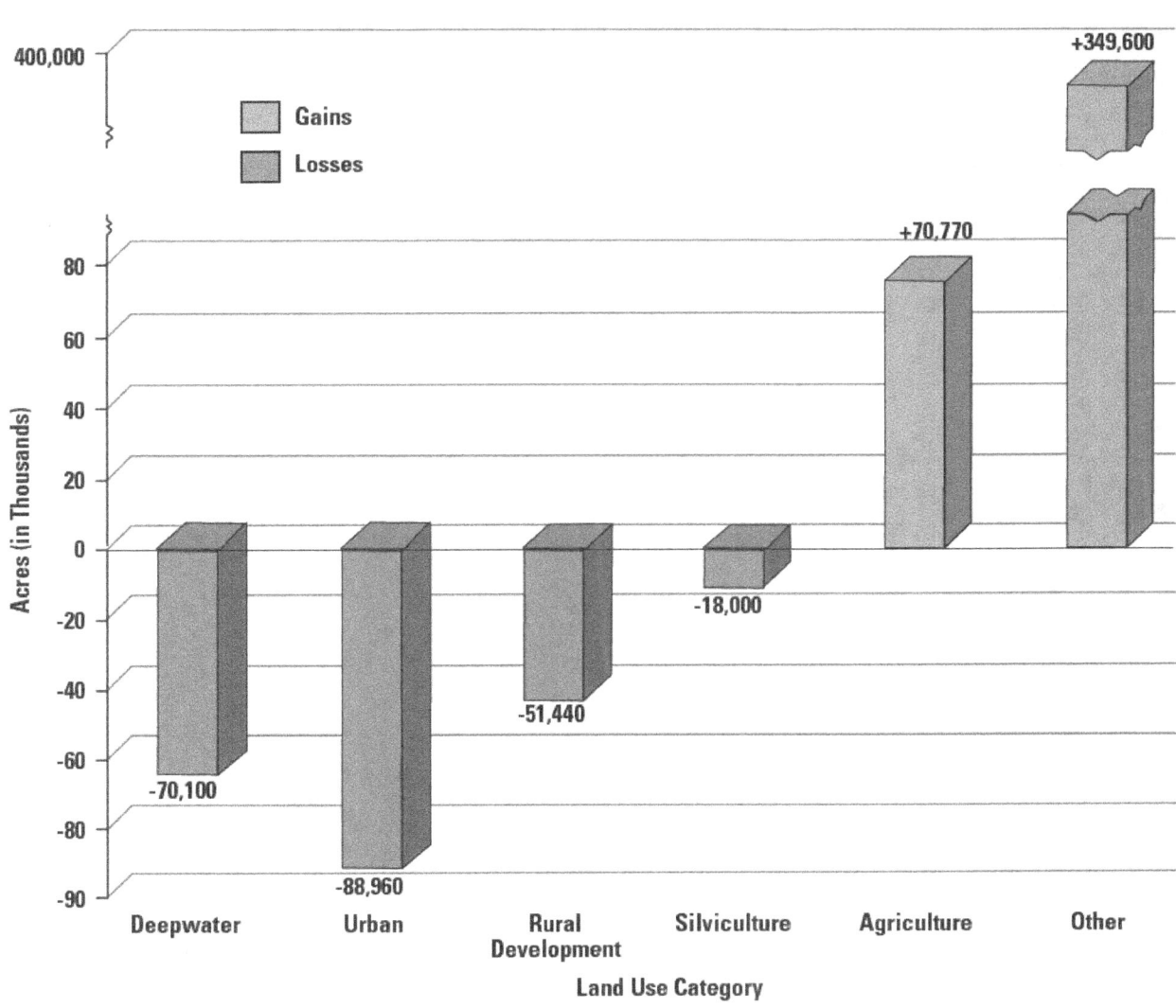

Figure 27. Wetlands gained or lost from upland categories and deepwater, 1998 to 2004.

Intertidal Estuarine and Marine Wetland Resources

Three major categories of estuarine and marine wetlands were included in this study: estuarine intertidal emergents (salt and brackish water marshes), estuarine shrub wetlands (mangrove swamps or mangles and other salt tolerant woody species) and estuarine and marine intertidal non-vegetated wetlands. This latter category included exposed coastal beaches subject to tidal flooding, shallow water sand bars, tidal flats, tidally exposed shoals and sand spits.

The vegetated components of the estuarine and marine systems are among the most biologically productive aquatic ecosystems in the world (Kennish 2004). Wetlands along the nation's coastline have provided valuable resources and supported large sections of the nation's economy (USEPA 2004). Wetlands have also provided opportunities for recreation and supported commercially valuable fish and crustacean populations. Estuarine and wetland dependent fish and shellfish species accounted for about 75 percent of the total annual seafood harvest in the United States (Weber 1995). In the Gulf of Mexico, coastal waters attracted millions of sport fishermen and beach users as tourism in the Gulf coast states contributed over $20 billion to the nation's economy (USEPA 1999). The importance of both estuarine and freshwater wetlands to fish populations, and sport and commercial fishing cannot be overemphasized. This link between wetlands and aquatic species includes ecological processes that are important for maintaining food webs, land and water interactions, and environmental quality.[8] Wetland loss and its effect on fish populations are among the many issues forcing a re-evaluation of activities on the landscape (NOAA 2001).

Estuarine and marine wetlands have been particularly susceptible to the various stressors resulting from rapid population growth and development within the coastal watersheds nationwide (Kennish

---
[8] The importance of wetlands to fish populations is discussed in the insert section "*Wetlands and Fish.*"

2004). From the 1950s to 1970s, estuarine wetlands were dredged and filled extensively for residential and commercial development and for navigation (Hefner 1986). To help conserve the nation's valuable coastal resources, numerous measures have been taken to protect estuarine and marine resources. Since the mid 1970s, many of the nation's shoreline habitats have been protected either by regulation or public ownership. These mechanisms, in combination with outreach and educational efforts, have been responsible for reducing intertidal wetlands losses in Florida (Dahl 2005).

This study estimated that in 2004 there were slightly more than 5.3 million acres (2.1 million ha) of marine and estuarine wetlands in the conterminous United States. Eighty six percent of that total area was vegetated wetland (Figure 28). Collectively, intertidal wetlands declined by an estimated 28,416 ac (11,580 ha) between 1998 and 2004. Estuarine vegetated wetlands declined by an estimated 32,400 acres (13,120 ha) between 1998 and 2004. Estuarine non-vegetated wetlands experienced a net gain of an estimated 4,000 ac (1,620 ha); marine intertidal shorelines declined by 1,900 ac (770 ha).

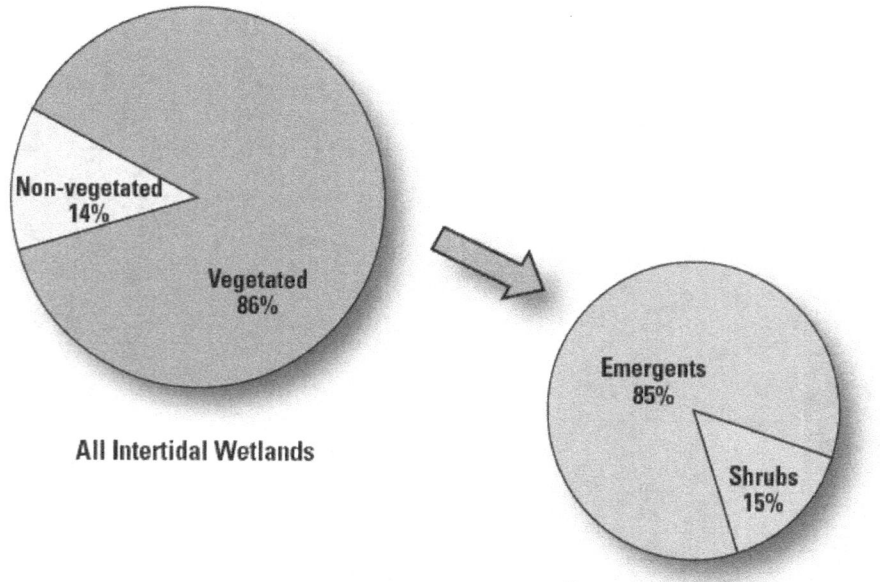

All Intertidal Wetlands

Non-vegetated 14%

Vegetated 86%

Estuarine Vegetated Wetlands

Emergents 85%

Shrubs 15%

Figure 28. Composition of marine and estuarine intertidal wetlands, 2004.

The changes that occurred between 1998 and 2004 in estuarine and marine wetlands are shown in Table 3. The largest acreage change was an estimated net loss of 33,230 acres (13,450 ha) of estuarine emergent wetland. The greatest percent change was a decline of 1.4 percent of marine intertidal wetland.

The overriding factor in the decline of estuarine and marine wetlands was loss of emergent salt marsh to open saltwater systems (Figure 29). This was due to natural and man-induced activities such as dredging, water control, and commercial and recreational boat traffic[9]. The losses of estuarine emergents exceeded the total net loss of all other intertidal estuarine and marine wetlands combined.

[9] Losses reported here were prior to the hurricanes of 2005. The Fish and Wildlife Service is preparing to conduct follow-up studies to reassess wetland changes along the Gulf Coast.

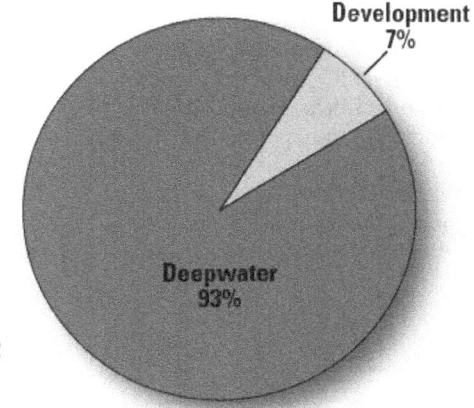

Figure 29. Estimated percent loss of intertidal estuarine and marine wetlands to deepwater and development, 1998 to 2004.

Development 7%

Deepwater 93%

Table 3. Changes to estuarine and marine wetlands, 1998 to 2004. The coefficient of variation (CV) for each entry (expressed as a percentage) is given in parentheses.

Wetland Category	Area, In Thousands of Acres				
	Estimated Area, 1998	Estimated Area, 2004	Gain or Loss, 1998–2004	Change (In Percent)	Area (as Percent) of All Intertidal Wetland, 2004
Marine Intertidal	130.4 (20.2)	128.6 (20.5)	−1.9 (68.7)	−1.4	2.4
Estuarine Unconsolidated Shore	563.2 (10.8)	567.5 (10.4)	4.3 *		10.7
Estuarine Aquatic Bed	30.8 (27.1)	32.4 (26.0)	1.6 (63.6)		0.6
Marine and Estuarine Intertidal Non-Vegetated	724.5 (9.8)	728.5 (9.5)	4.0 *	0.5	13.7
Estuarine Emergent	3,922.8 (4.2)	3,889.5 (4.2)	−33.2 (31.8)		73.4
Estuarine Shrub	681.4 (12.5)	682.2 (12.5)	0.8 *		12.9
Estuarine Intertidal Vegetated[1]	4,604.2 (4.0)	4,571.7 (4.0)	−32.4 (32.6)	−0.7	86.3
Changes in Coastal Deepwater area, 1998–2004					
Estuarine Subtitdal	17,680.5 (2.2)	17,717.8 (2.2)	37.3 (40.8)	—	—

*Statistically unreliable.

[1] Includes the categories: Estuarine Emergent and Estuarine Shrub.

Excludes marine and estuarine wetlands of California, Oregon and Washington.

Percent coefficient of variation was expressed as (standard deviation/mean) x (100).

Marine and Estuarine Beaches, Tidal Bars, Flats and Shoals

Sand, mud or rock beaches, bars and shoals along the interface with tidal saltwater composed the non-vegetated intertidal wetlands (Figure 30). These areas were subject to dramatic changes resulting from coastal storms, hurricanes, tidal surge, sea level rise, sediment deposition or various forms of artificial manipulation during this study period.

Ecologically, these wetlands are important to a variety of fish and wildlife species. Open sandy beach habitats are particularly important to nesting, foraging and loafing waterbirds (Kushlan *et al.* 2002) (Figure 31 and 32). The green sea turtle (*Chelonia mydas*) and the loggerhead sea turtle (*Caretta caretta*) also use sandy beaches for nesting sites. Shallow water coastal flats are important for sport fish such as the sand sea trout (*Cynoscion arenarius*), bonefish (*Albuta vulpes*), and snook (*Centropomus undecimalis*).

There were an estimated 728,540 acres (294,960 ha) of intertidal non-vegetated wetlands in 2004. This study found that from 1998 to 2004 (Table 4) marine intertidal beaches declined by 1,900 acres (770 ha), a 1.4 percent decline. This was very similar to the rate of decline observed from 1986 to 1997, when marine beaches declined 1.7 percent.

Estuarine bars, flats and shoals (Figure 33) increased in area over the same timeframe. There was an estimated increase of 4,300 acres (1,740 ha). This increase was largely at the expense of estuarine emergent salt marsh which was sloughed into deeper water bays and sounds. Land subsidence, saltwater intrusion and coastal erosion processes may have contributed to these changes.

Intertidal non-vegetated wetland changes to urban and other forms of upland development were not statistically significant.

Figure 30 . Non-vegetated tidal flats grade into sparsely vegetated beach ridges. These areas are important for a variety of birds, sea turtles and other marine life. Florida, 2000.

Figure 31. Intertidal marine beaches provide important habitat for shorebirds. These types of wetlands declined by 1.4 percent between 1998 and 2004. Coastal Louisiana, 2005. Photo by J. Harner, USGS.

Figure 32. The black-necked stilt (*Himantopus mexicanus*) inhabits mud flats, pools, back water beaches, brackish ponds of saltwater marshes and other wetland habitats. Photo courtesy of FWS.

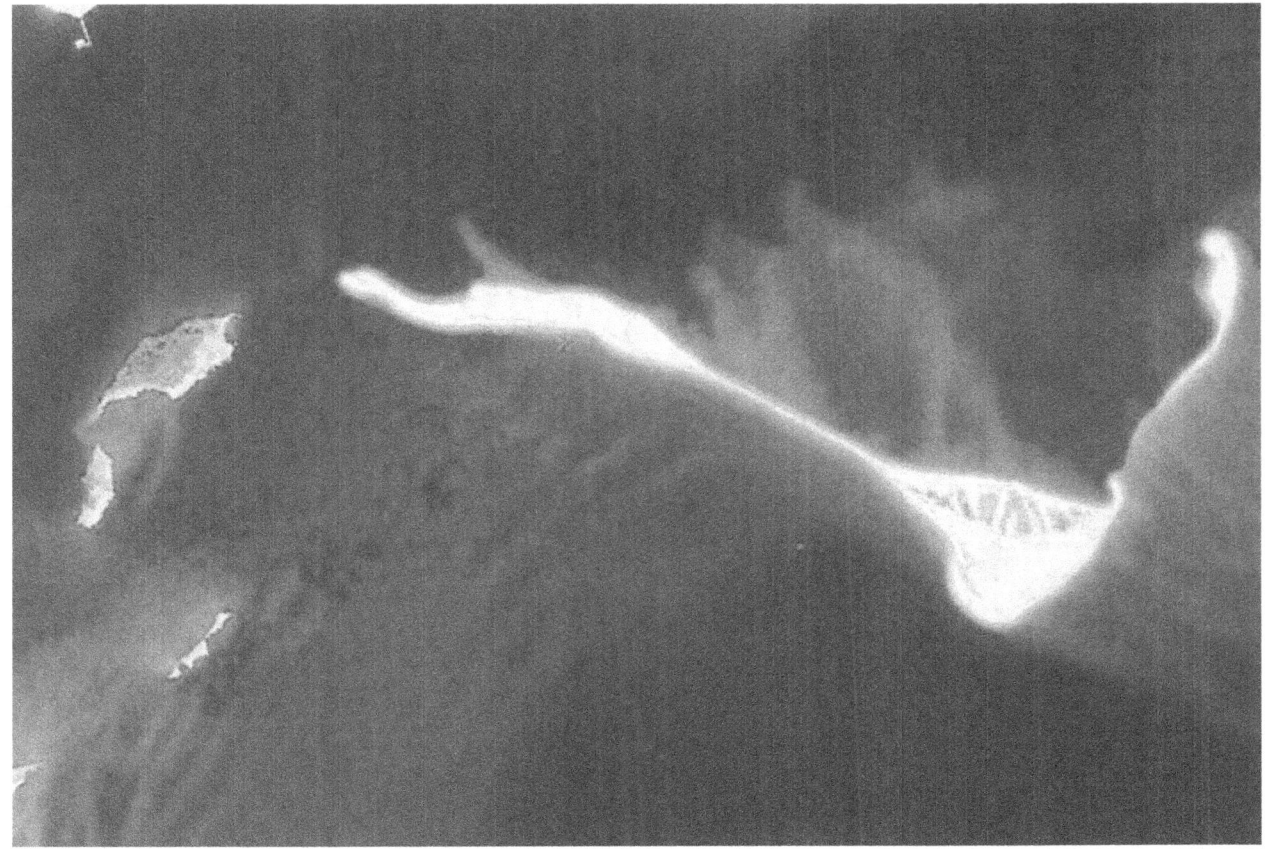

Figure 33. New shoals and sand bars are continually forming in shallow water areas. This image shows a new feature (brightest white areas) off from the coast of Virginia, 2004.

Estuarine Emergent Wetlands

Estuarine emergent wetlands (synonymous with the term "salt marsh") were found close to the shoreline and were associated with estuaries, lagoons, embayments, sounds and coastal barriers (Figure 34). Salinities ranged from hypersaline to oligohaline (Cowardin *et al.* 1979). The coastal plain of the southeastern Atlantic and Gulf States supported expansive areas of intertidal estuarine wetlands, particularly emergent salt marsh. These marshes support diverse animal life and are extremely productive and ecologically important features on the coastal landscape. The abundance and distribution of individual species of both animals and plants are influenced by physical conditions including salinity, water depth, tidal fluctuation and temperature variations (Chabreck 1988).

There were an estimated 3,889,500 acres (1,574,700 ha) of estuarine emergent salt marsh wetland in 2004.

Estuarine emergent wetland declined by 33,230 acres (13,450 ha) between 1998 and 2004. This represented a loss of 0.9 percent of this wetland type. The average annual rate of estuarine emergent loss was 5,540 acres (2,240 ha). This rate of loss was consistent with the rate of salt marsh loss recorded from 1986 to 1997 (Dahl 2000). Urban and rural development activities, and the conversion of wetlands to other upland land uses, accounted for an estimated loss of 1,732 acres (700 ha) or about 3.0 percent of all losses of estuarine emergent wetland. Most of the losses of estuarine emergent wetland were due to loss to deep salt water and occurred in coastal Louisiana (Figure 35).

Numerous restoration and rehabilitation projects have been undertaken in Louisiana as part of the Coastal Wetlands Planning, Protection and Restoration Act of 1990, to begin the process of slowing the rate of wetland loss in that region (Zinn and Copeland 2002). Despite these efforts, the rate of estuarine wetland loss has remained constant since the mid 1980s. Projects undertaken in Louisiana may have restored functional value of some wetlands. Other restoration efforts might have been directed toward freshwater wetlands elsewhere within "coastal" proximity but outside of the estuarine and marine systems.

Figure 34. High altitude infrared photograph of salt marsh (darker mottles) offshore from coastal Georgia, 2004.

Figure 35. Estuarine emergent losses as observed in this study along the Atlantic and Gulf of Mexico. Inset shows close up of Louisiana where most losses occurred between 1998 and 2004.

Estuarine Emergent Wetland Loss

- 0–25 Acres
- 26–75 Acres
- 76–150 Acres
- 151–300 Acres

53

Estimates of wetland loss from this study were contrasted with other estimates of wetland loss in Louisiana as seen in Table 4. Geographic dissimilarities and terminology differences including "coastal" versus "estuarine," "wetland" versus "land loss," and temporal differences accounted for some of the discrepancies. It is clear that there has been confusion over the region included (where), types of wetland and/or upland included in the estimates (what) and the timeframe of when losses occurred (when). This study measured changes in marine and estuarine wetlands from 1998 to 2004 as described earlier.

One or more of several interrelated factors may have contributed to the loss of estuarine emergent wetland, including: deficiencies in sediment deposition, canals and artificially created waterways, wave erosion, land subsidence, and salt water intrusion causing marsh disintegration. In recognizing that human activities have affected wetlands in Louisiana, Williams *et al.* (1995) cited an extensive system of dredged canals and flood-control structures constructed to facilitate hydrocarbon exploration and production as well as commercial and recreational boat traffic that had enabled salt water to intrude from the Gulf of Mexico as major factors in wetland loss.

Coastal storms often have had a role in destabilizing salt marsh substrates by washing away sediment with wind driven floodwaters (Chabreck 1988). Estimates of estuarine emergent area reported here, were made prior to Hurricane Katrina and Rita during the summer of 2005. These storm events may have further exacerbated vegetated marsh losses by creating open water pockets or lakes to replace vegetated wetlands in St. Bernard and Plaquemines Parishes, Louisiana (USGS 2005b).

Estuarine emergent wetlands have been restored elsewhere in the country. An estimated 2,540 acres were reclaimed from freshwater wetlands through projects such as the Dande Meadows Salt Marsh Project in Massachusetts. This project restored natural salt marsh that had been converted into a freshwater hayfield during colonial times (Coastal America 2003). Small to moderate scale projects have been undertaken within the National Estuarine Research Reserve System as well. There, the focus has been on restoring salt marsh and seagrass beds where ecological functions have declined (Kennish 2004).

Table 4. Contrasting different estimates of wetland loss in Louisiana.

Habitat Description	Estimated Loss Rate	Normalized[1] Loss Rate (Hectares per Year)	Source
Coastal marsh	50 acres/day	7,390 ha	Moorman (2005) Ducks Unlimited Southern Region
Coast and wetlands	25 sq. mi./yr	6,480 ha	Louisiana State University (2005)
Wetlands of coastal Louisiana	50 sq. mi./yr	12,960 ha	Louisiana Geological Survey and EPA (1987)
Louisiana's wetlands	75 sq. km/yr	7,500 ha	Williams (1995) USGS—Marine and Coastal Geology Program
Louisiana's wetlands	16,000 to 25,000 acres/yr	6,480 to 10,120 ha	National Marine Fisheries Service (www.nmfs.noaa.gov/habitat)(2005)
Coastal land	25 to 35 sq. mi/yr	6,480 to 9,070 ha	Tulane University (2004)
Marsh	40 sq. mi./yr	10,360 ha	USGS, National Wetland Research Center (2005)
Estuarine and Marine emergent wetland	5,500 acres/yr	2,240 ha	This Study

[1]Scaled to 365 days and expressed as hectares.

Conversion factors:

Square mile = 640 acres

Hectare = 2.47 acres

Square kilometer = 247 acres

Estuarine Shrub Wetlands

Among the most notable components of the estuarine shrub wetland category are mangrove swamps. The geographic extent of mangroves has been influenced by cold temperatures, hurricanes, and human induced stressors (Spalding *et al.* 1997). Florida has always been the primary location of mangrove wetlands in the United States. Mangrove species are uniquely adapted to saline environments and ecologically mangroves have supported a diversity of wildlife (Odum and McIvor 1990). Mangrove communities and surrounding waters of south Florida support more than 220 species of fish, 24 species of reptiles and amphibians, 18 mammals and 181 bird species (U.S. Fish and Wildlife Service 1996) (Figure 36).

Mitsch and Gosselink (1993) indicated that the northern-most extent of black mangrove (*Avicennia geminans*) occurred at about 30 degrees N. latitude. Although scattered stands of mangrove shrubs have been found along the north coast of the Gulf of Mexico (Odum and McIvor 1990), these wetlands have been exposed to freezing temperatures that greatly reduced their number and distribution. Estuarine shrub wetlands may have included woody species other than mangroves. Other salt-tolerant or invasive woody plants in these northern wetlands included false willow (*Baccharis angustifolia*), saltbush (*Baccharis halimifolia*), buttonwood (*Conocarpus erectus*), bay cedar (*Suriana maritina*) and Brazilian pepper (*Schinus terebinthifolius*).

There were an estimated 682,200 acres (276,190 ha) of estuarine shrub wetland in 2004. This estimate represented a gain of about 800 acres (320 ha). Most of this gain came from areas formerly classified as estuarine emergent wetland. The acreage estimates of estuarine shrub wetlands have been steady or increased slightly over the past two decades.

The long term trend in all intertidal wetlands, estuarine vegetated and estuarine non-vegetated categories is shown in Figure 37 A-C. Estuarine vegetated wetlands have continued to decline over time as losses to the estuarine emergent category have overshadowed the small gains to estuarine shrub wetlands.

Figure 36. Pelican Island, Florida, the nation's first National Wildlife Refuge is located in the Indian River Lagoon, a biologically diverse estuary of mangrove islands, salt marsh, and maritime hammocks. Photo courtesy of the FWS.

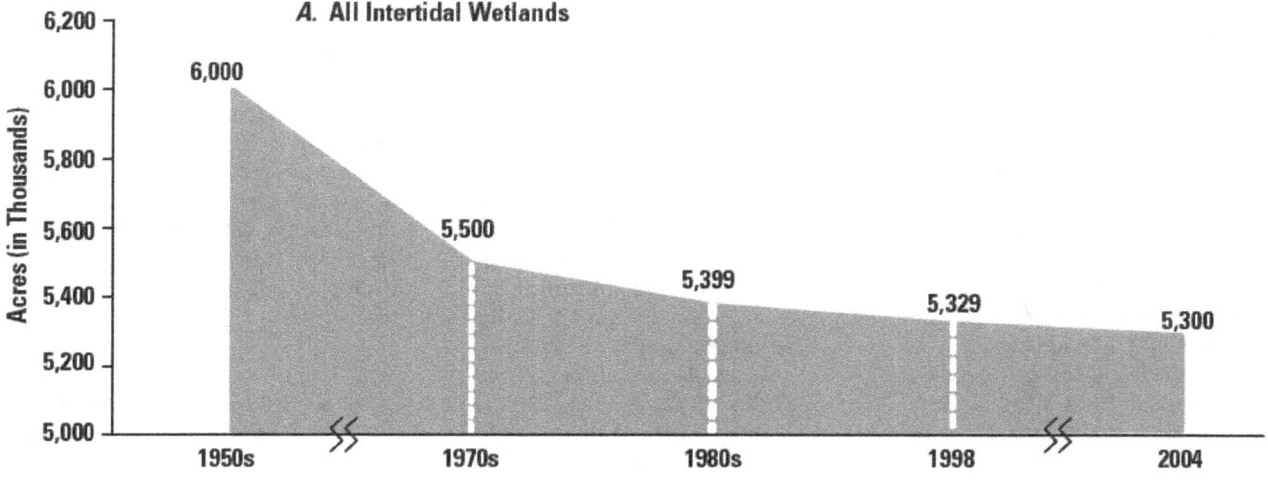

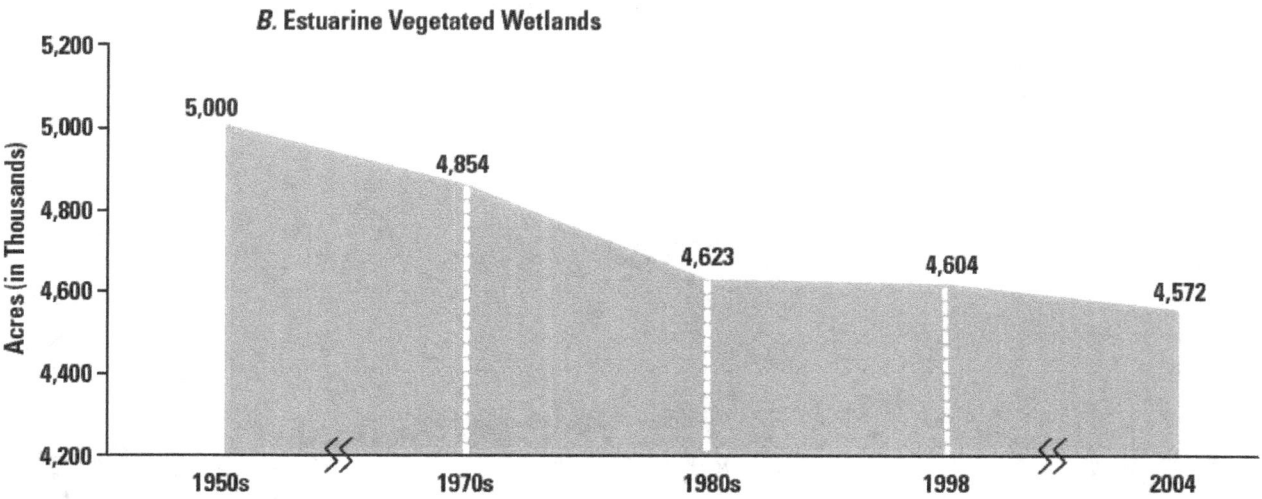

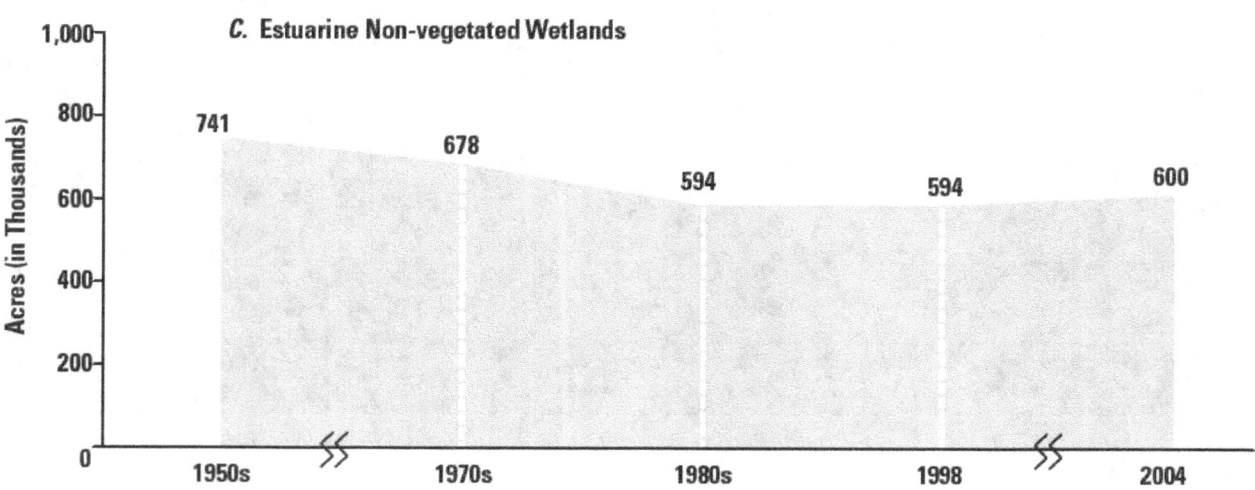

Figure37 A–C. Long-term trends in A) all intertidal wetlands, B) estuarine vegetated wetlands and C) estuarine non-vegetated wetlands, 1950s to 2004.

Wetlands and Fish

Formed in 1922, The Izaak Walton League is one of the nation's oldest conservation organizations to address deteriorating conditions of America's top fishing streams. The League is named for the 17th-century English angler-conservationist who wrote the literary classic "The Compleat Angler." Since 1992, the League has been restoring wetlands and streams, establishing wildlife refuges and parks, and teaching outdoor ethics to outdoor enthusiasts, sportsmen and conservationists. League members recognize the importance of wetlands and the role they play in supporting fish species and angling opportunities throughout the United States.

Fish and seafood provide the largest source of protein for people across the world. The worldwide fish harvest has surpassed cattle production and poultry farming as the primary source of animal protein (FAO 1987). The United States consumes more than 4 billion tons of fish and shellfish every year—an average of 16 pounds per person (National Marine Fisheries Service 2004). Additionally, about 34 million people in the United States fish for recreation (USFWS 2001).

America's coastal and freshwater fish populations are currently facing an unprecedented decline. Since 1900, 123 aquatic freshwater species have become extinct in North America. Of the 822 native freshwater fish species in the United States, 39 percent are at risk of extinction (Fisheries and Water Resources Policy Committee 2004) and 72 percent of freshwater mussels are imperiled (USFWS 2004a). Additionally, the world's catch of ocean fish has been steadily falling since 1989, with 13 of the 17 most productive fisheries currently facing steep declines. Several factors have contributed to this decline, including over-fishing and pollution. However, the rate at which America's fish populations are plummeting is largely due to the loss and alteration of their aquatic habitats.

At one time, the conterminous United States contained more than 220 million acres of wetland habitat. Although government programs, conservation organizations, and private individuals are slowing wetland loss and restoring degraded wetlands, the total wetland acreage in the lower 48 states has declined to the current 107 million acres. The nation's wetlands are vital to fish health. Wetlands provide an essential link in the life cycle of 75 percent of the fish and shellfish commercially harvested in the United States, and up to 90 percent of the recreational fish catch. Wetlands provide clean water, a consistent food supply, shelter, and nursery areas for both marine and freshwater species. Salmon, winter flounder, and largemouth bass, among others, depend on healthy wetlands.

Largemouth bass *(Micropterus salmoides)* is the most popular game fish in the United States. Shallow marshes at the edges of lakes and floodplain wetlands of large, slow moving rivers are favorite habitats for the largemouth bass. Stocking largemouth in smaller ponds and recreational lakes has been a common sport fishery management practice in many states. Image courtesy of FWS.

By providing essential habitat and other benefits to fish populations, wetlands play a crucial role in maintaining the long-term health of our aquatic resources and contribute to economic prosperity. Sport fishing is responsible for a multi-million dollar industry that supports television shows, magazines, fishing clubs and organizations, tackle and boat manufacturing and fishing tournaments held nationwide. In total, wetland-dependent species make up 71 percent of the commercial and recreational fisheries, supporting an industry that contributes $111 billion annually to our national economy and employs two million people (Fisheries and Water Resources Policy Committee 2004).

How Wetlands Support Healthy Fish Populations

Clean Water

Wetlands have been termed "nature's kidneys" because they filter and purify our streams, rivers and waterways.

Wetlands slow down moving water, allowing sediments suspended in the water to gradually settle to the ground. Cattails (*Typha spp.*) and other ermergent and submergent vegetation help remove dangerous heavy metals, like copper and arsenic, from the water column. Other pollutants, like lead, mercury and pesticides, are trapped by soil particles and are gradually broken down by microbes. Wetland plants and microorganisms also filter out and absorb excess nutrients that can result from fertilizer application, manure, and

Northern Pike (*Esox lucius*) and Muskellunge (*Esox masquinongy*) are found in heavily vegetated wetlands in the shallow waters along the edges of lakes and large rivers. These are some of North America's most important freshwater game fish species. Image courtesy of FWS.

municipal sewage. When large amounts of nitrogen and phosphorus enter our waterways, a massive overgrowth of algae can occur, depleting dissolved oxygen levels and stressing fish populations. Wetlands can remove more than half of the phosphorous and 75 percent of the nitrogen out of the incoming water flow (U.S. Environmental Protection Agency 1993) This natural filtering ability reduces the negative impacts of agricultural and municipal run-off, and it lessesns the need to implement costly technological solutions. For example, if half of all the existing wetlands were destroyed, it would cost over $62 billion per year to upgrade sewage treatment plants to handle all the extra pollution (Environmental Defense Fund and World Wildlife Fund 1992) Some types of wetlands are so good at this filtration function that environmental managers construct similar artificial wetlands to treat storm water and wastewater near urban centers.

Sockeye salmon (*Oncorhynchus nerka*) spend their life in open sea, but return to freshwater streams to spawn. These fish support one of the most important commercial fisheries on the Pacific coast. Image courtesy of FWS.

Food Production

The diverse conditions found in wetlands allow many different types of organisms, some with highly specialized adaptations, to co-exist within a small area. This wide range of species is supported by the extraordinary rates of plant productivity that characterize most wetland habitats. Some fish species benefit directly by feeding on plant parts, while other fish eat the small insects and crustaceans that live on plants. Some fish prefer wetland plant material that forms the detritus found on the bottom of aquatic habitats. Wetlands indirectly nourish the entire aquatic system when this rich organic matter is washed downstream, where it benefits fish living many miles away in the open ocean. Menhaden (*Brevoortia tyrannus*), for example, rely upon detritus for a full third of their diet, even though they live far from the wetlands where it is produced.

Rainbow trout, *Onchorhynchus mykiss* Image courtesy of FWS.

Spawning and Nursery Areas

Fish eggs and young fish have different needs. Some fish live in other habitats as adults and return to wetlands to lay their eggs. Defenseless and immobile eggs can be hidden from predators by underwater vegetation.

Black Crappie (*Pomoxis nigromaculatus*) and White Crappie (*Pomoxis annularis*) use submerged vegetation and brush as spawning habitats. Image courtesy of FWS.

Wetland plants and detritus provide a surface for some fish to attach their eggs. When the eggs hatch, the vegetation becomes both a protective cover and a food source. Young fish dart into the wetland vegetation to hide, while the juvenile stages of bay scallops, hard clams, and some other shellfish cling to salt marsh vegetation and seagrasses for several weeks before settling on the bottom. Most shrimp harvested in the Gulf of Mexico depend on salt marshes for nurseries, yet this latest study reports that these salt marsh wetlands continued to decline by over 33,000 acres (13,450 ha) between 1998 and 2004.

Refuge

Both adult and juvenile fish use wetlands to hide from predators. Thick plant growth can visually confuse predators and disguise small fish. Juvenile muskellunge, northern pike and other and mottled colored fish can hide by blending in with surrounding aquatic vegetation. Dense vegetation and shallow water prevent many pelagic predators from entering coastal marshes and freshwater wetlands fringing lakes and rivers. Anchovies (*Engraulis mordax*), juvenile snook (*Centropomus undecimalis*), and juvenile spotted seatrout (*Cynoscion nebulosus*) dart into the intertwining root systems of mangrove wetlands to escape larger predators. The root systems of trees and shrubs in floodplain wetlands allow stream banks to hang over the water, providing protective habitat for Chinook salmon (*Oncorhynchus tshawytscha*), cutthroat trout (*Oncorhynchus clarki*), and other fish.

Fish also use wetlands to seek refuge from changes in water level, velocity, or bad weather. Coho salmon rely on the calmer waters of forested wetlands adjacent to streams to escape fast currents during winter floods. Wetland plants help maintain appropriate levels of oxygen in the water and keep temperatures cool for aquatic life.

Management and conservation for all aquatic resources are a shared responsibility. Agencies, organizations and individuals must continue to be involved in wetlands and fisheries conservation activities to protect these important resources.

Leah Miller and Suzanne Zanelli, Izaak Walton League of America
www.iwla.org

Brook trout, *Salvelinus fontinalis*
Image courtesy of FWS.

Some of the information in this article was taken from the publication *Wetlands and Fish: Catch the Link*, produced by the Izaak Walton League and the National Marine Fisheries Service. You can download this publication at http://www.nmfs.noaa.gov/habitat/habitatconservation/publications/hcpub.htm

Photos courtesy of FWS.

Freshwater Wetland Resources

Freshwater, or palustrine, wetlands included forested wetlands, freshwater emergents, shrubs, and freshwater ponds less than 20 acres (8 ha). Freshwater wetlands have been known by many common names such as swamp, bog, fen, marsh, swale, oxbow and wet meadow. Ninety five percent of all wetland area in the conterminous United States was freshwater. In 2004, there were an estimated 102.5 million acres (41.5 million ha) of freshwater wetlands. Table 5 summarized the changes in freshwater wetlands between 1998 and 2004.

Gains and Losses in Freshwater Wetlands

There have been large shifts between the freshwater wetland types and uplands. Most wetland loss (e.g. drainage, fills) and wetland creation and restoration that occurred between 1998 and 2004 involved some type of freshwater wetland.

All net gains in wetland area took place in freshwater systems. Overall, the estimated net gain in freshwater wetland area between 1998 and 2004 was 220,200 acres (89,140 ha).

Freshwater wetland gains resulted from wetland restorations and the creation of numerous freshwater ponds (Figure 38). The status of freshwater ponds is discussed later in this section.

Wetland Restoration—Between 1987 and 1990, programs to restore wetlands under the 1985 Food Security Act added about 90,000 acres (36,400 ha) to the nation's wetland base (Dahl and Johnson 1991). Between 1986 and 1997, there was a net gain of wetland from "other" uplands of about 180,000 acres (72,900 ha) (Dahl, 2000). During those previous study periods wetland restoration and creation was not sufficient to overcome wetland losses. From 1986 to 1997, there was a deficit between freshwater wetland losses and gains of about 630,000 acres (255,100 ha). This was due to freshwater wetland conversion to upland land uses (Dahl 2000).

The federal government works cooperatively with landowners, states, tribes and communities through a number of programs to achieve restoration, protection and improvement (see Appendix D). One of the primary wetland restoration programs of the Fish and Wildlife Service is the Partners for Fish and Wildlife Program. This program has been available to private landowners and has provided both technical and financial assistance to restore wetlands and other fish and wildlife habitats. Examples of restoration projects include restoring wetlands, planting native trees and grasses, removal of exotics, prescribed burning, reconstruction of stream habitat and reestablishment of fish passageways (*www.fws.gov/partners 2005*).

Another restoration program of the Fish and Wildlife Service is the North American Waterfowl Management Plan (NAWMP), a public-private approach to managing waterfowl populations. Cooperation and coordination with partners and stakeholders is key to implementation of NAWMP

Table 5 Changes in freshwater wetland area between 1998 and 2004. The coefficient of variation (CV) for each entry (expressed as a percentage) is given in parentheses.

Freshwater Wetland Category	Area, in Thousands of Acres			Change (in Percent)
	Estimated Area, 1998	Estimated Area, 2004	Change, 1998–2004	
Freshwater Emergent	26,289.6 (8.0)	26, 147.0 (8.0)	−142.6 *	−0.5
Freshwater Forested	51,483.1 (2.8)	52,031.4 (2.8)	548.2 (56.1)	1.1
Freshwater Shrub	18,542.2 (4.1)	17.641.4 (4.3)	−900.8 (34.2)	−4.9
Freshwater Vegetated Wetlands	96,314.9 (3.0)	95,819.8 (3.0)	−495.1 (35.0)	−0.5
Ponds[1]	5,534.3 (3.7)	6,229.6 (3.5)	695.4 (13.1)	12.6
Miscellaneous Types[2]	384.4 (16.3)	404.3 (15.6)	19.9 (54.2)	5.2
Freshwater Non-Vegetated	5,918.7 (3.7)	6,633.9 (3.5)	715.3 (12.8)	12.1
All Freshwater Wetlands	102,233.6 (2.9)	102,453.7 (2.8)	220.2 (77.3)	0.2

*Statistically unreliable.

[1]Includes the categories: Palustrine Aquatic Bed and Palustrine Unconsolidated Bottom.

[2]Palustrine Unconsolidated Shore.

Percent coefficient of variation was expressed as (standard deviation/mean) x (100).

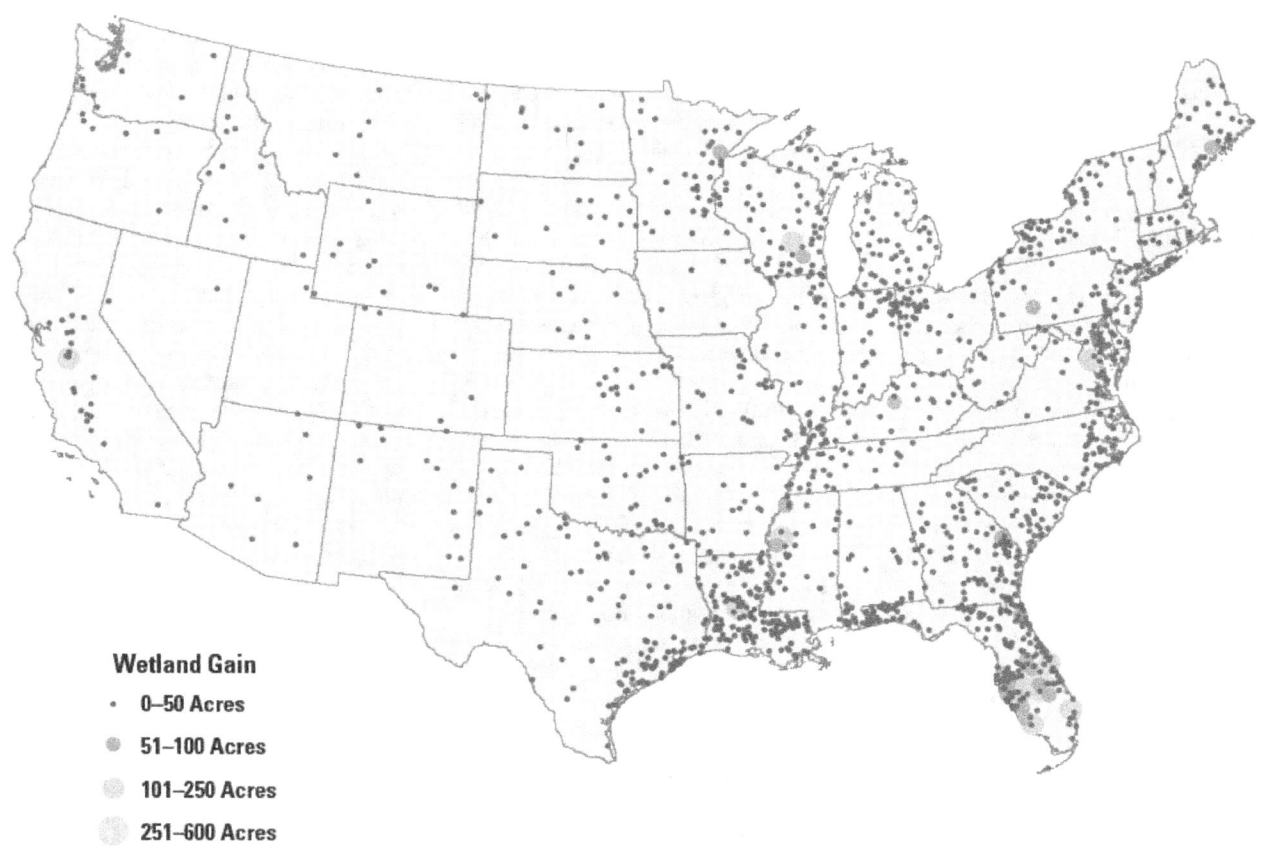

Wetland Gain

· 0–50 Acres

● 51–100 Acres

● 101–250 Acres

● 251–600 Acres

Figure 38. Approximate density and distribution of freshwater wetland gains identified in the samples of this study.

Figure 39. A tile drained wetland basin has been restored. Ohio, 2005.

and to successfully protect and conserve waterfowl through habitat protection, restoration, and enhancement. The habitat objectives of NAWMP identify key waterfowl habitat areas and call for their conservation and protection. Working with partners and cooperators NAWMP seeks to enhance, protect and restore wetlands that contribute to those waterfowl habitat objectives.

Over the past decade, many agencies and organizations have been actively involved in wetland restoration, enhancement or creation. Many beneficial projects have been completed by federal, state, local and private organizations and citizens. Some of these projects have involved removal of invasive species in wetlands, restoration of hydrology to partially drained habitats, selective plantings and reestablishment of vegetation, improved wetland quality and other

habitat improvement activities. These wetland enhancement projects have not contributed area gains to the wetland base and were not part of this study.

An estimated 564,300 acres (228,460 ha) of wetlands were restored on agricultural lands between 1998 and 2004. However, the loss of wetlands to agricultural land use was responsible for an estimated 488,200 acres (197,650 ha) during the same period. The net gain of about 76,100 acres (30,800 ha) did not tell the entire story of wetland restored or created from agricultural land. As lands became enrolled in retirement or conservation programs, they were subsequently re-classified to the upland "other" land use category (e.g. there were no identifiable land use characteristics). Thus, some areas attributed to wetland restoration were actually

conversions of upland agricultural land to the upland "other" category.

Replacement of wetland with a structure (house or office building) or development resulting from urban or suburban infrastructure (roads and bridges), usually constituted an irreversible loss (Ainslie 2002). It follows that most restoration and creation of freshwater wetlands would have to come from the agricultural sector or undeveloped lands classified as "other." The "other" lands category also included many conservation lands such as undeveloped land on National Wildlife Refuges, in state game management areas or preserves, idle lands or land in retirement programs planted to permanent cover, as well as national and state park lands (Figure 40). This trend of gaining wetland acres from the "other" land use category was seen in the previous era study where 180,000 acres (72,900 ha) of "other" land was converted to wetland (Dahl 2000).

Figure 40. Wetland restoration (freshwater emergent) on land previously classified as upland "other." Indiana, 2005. Photo by M. Bergeson.

The Council on Environmental Quality (2005) provided an assessment of wetland restoration and creation by federal programs that showed 58 percent of the acreage was attributed to agricultural conservation and technical assistance programs and about 32 percent was attributed to other federal initiatives such as those completed on conservation lands.

The National Resources Inventory conducted by the U.S. Department of Agriculture estimated a total net change of 263,000 acres (106,470 ha) in freshwater and estuarine wetlands on nonfederal land from 1997 to 2003 (USDA—NRCS 2004). Despite subtle differences and nuances between that study and this study and different timeframes, there was general agreement between the studies with regard to wetland trends due to agriculture.

Agricultural conservation programs were responsible for most of the gross wetland restoration acreage (Figure 41 and 42). Swampbuster and the Wetlands Reserve Program were two of the largest contributors, but other programs such as the Conservation Reserve, Farmed Wetlands Option and the Conservation Reserve Enhancement Programs also contributed (Zinn and Copeland 2002). Agricultural programs to promote pond construction also contributed to the increased freshwater pond acreage.

Private efforts to restore wetlands were also observed in the field. These included wetlands restored by private hunt clubs, community projects, and individual land owners (Figures 43A and B).

This study estimated that between 1998 and 2004, net wetland gains were 191,750 acres (77,630 ha). Estimates of restored wetland acreage from this study cannot be compared with those of other studies that used different definitions.

Figure 41. Wetland restoration attributed to agricultural conservation programs in the upper midwest, 2004. The wetland can be seen in the center with light green and white vegetation, darker irregular shape is surface water with vegetation.

Figure 42. A restored wetland basin. This basin had been drained and part used as a farm field (right) (A), the other portion remained a partially drained wetland (left) (B). Hydrology has been restored and the part on the right represented an acreage gain. Minnesota, 2005.

Figure 43 A. Private efforts to restore wetlands also contributed to the national acreage base. Western Minnesota, 2004. Photo by M. Watmough.

Figure 43B. Stone Lake, Wisconsin, 2005.

Wetlands Loss—Losses of freshwater wetlands were also numerous. Notable losses of freshwater vegetated wetlands occurred in the Prairie Pothole Region of eastern North and South Dakota, western Minnesota and Iowa. Losses were observed in Michigan, Wisconsin, Indiana, Ohio, North and South Carolina, Georgia, Florida, Louisiana and the vicinities around and including Houston, Texas and Memphis, Tennessee. Eighty five percent of all freshwater wetland losses were wetlands less than 5.0 acres (2.0 ha). Fifty two percent were wetlands less than 1.0 acre (0.4 ha). These data indicate that restorations helped ameliorate wetland losses however, some small wetlands or smaller portions of larger wetlands continue to be destroyed. Examples of wetland losses are shown in Figures 44 and 45.

Despite the net gains realized from restoration and creation projects, human induced wetland losses continued to affect the trends of freshwater vegetated wetlands. This study estimated that urban expansion and rural development were responsible for 61 percent of the total net wetland loss from 1998 to 2004. Areas of the country where this was most prevalent included the Gulf–Atlantic coastal plain, the Great Lakes states and the southeastern United States. Development conflicts with wetlands in rapidly growing areas of Florida were particularly evident (Figure 46). In some instances, these developments were also responsible

Figure 44. Examples of wetland loss. Fill being placed into a wetland pond in Ohio, 2005.

Figure 45. An emergent weland in rural Pennsylvania, 2005 in the process of being filled. Both examples in Figures 46 and 47 were attributed to Rural Development.

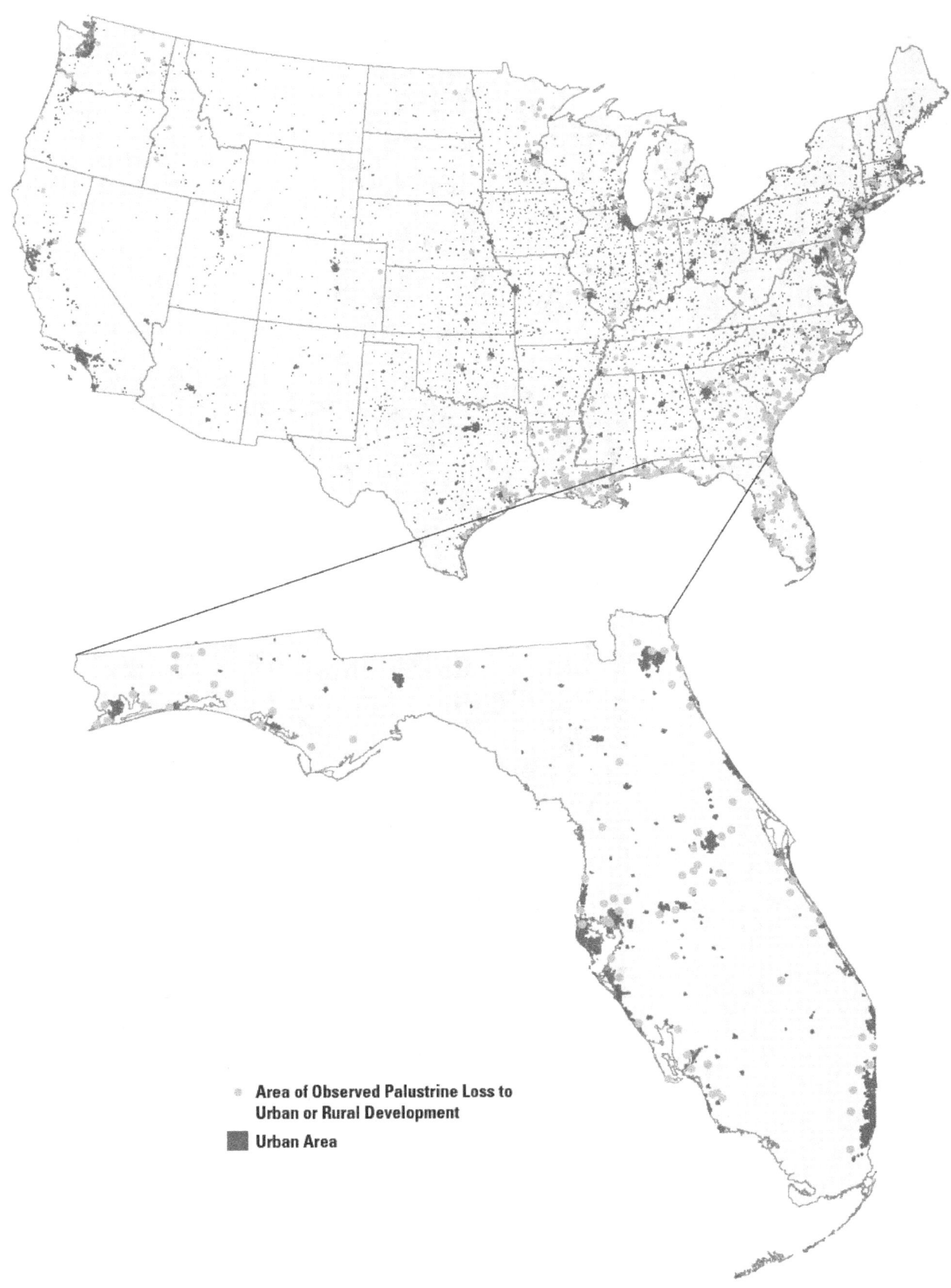

Figure 46. Areas experiencing wetland loss due to development, 1998 to 2004. Urban areas defined by the U.S. Geological Survey's National Atlas (original data 1:2,000,000 scale, updated 2005).

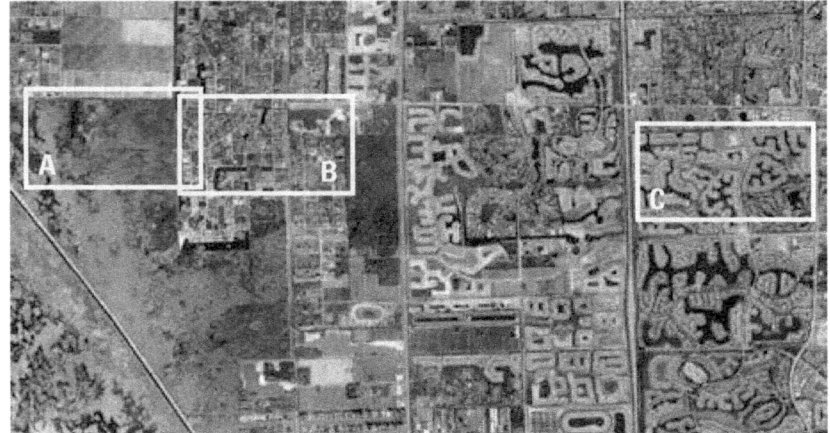

for the creation of residential lakes and ponds used for water retention and aesthetics. However, these open water wetlands often replaced vegetated freshwater wetlands (Figure 47A-C and overview) and were not an equivalent replacement for vegetated wetlands as discussed in a later section of this report.

Figure 47. Development in rapidly growing area of south Florida. Insets A–C enlarged from figure above. These photographs have been used as examples of wetland and land use trends. There is no evidence or implication that this represents future change.

A) Largely undeveloped area where vegetated wetland predominates.

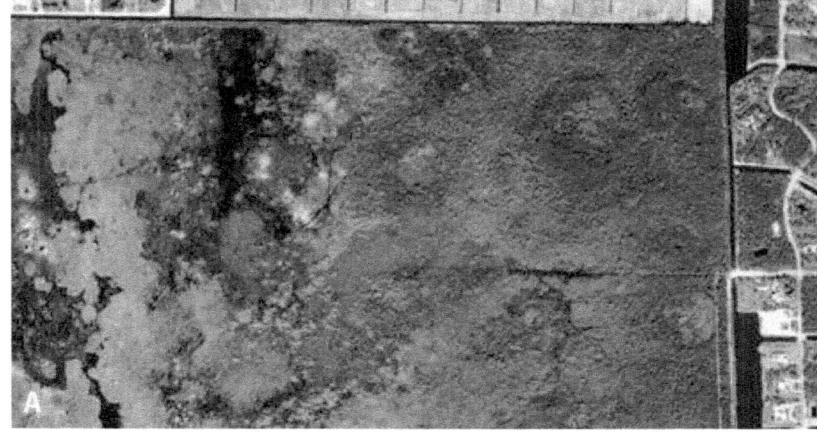

B) "Sparse" development. Surface waters have been channelized and retained in open water ponds.

C) Dense residential development. Surface waters are contained in artificial ponds and lakes.

The amount of freshwater vegetated wetlands lost has declined by about 17 percent when comparing results from the 1986 to 1997 study to this study. Losses of freshwater vegetated wetlands have steadily decreased since the mid 1970s estimates (Figure48).

Some restoration, creation and enhancement projects resulted from efforts to mitigate permitted wetland losses that occurred at a different site(s) (Figure 49). It was beyond the scope of this study to determine how effective such mitigation was in terms of an acre-for-acre replacement.

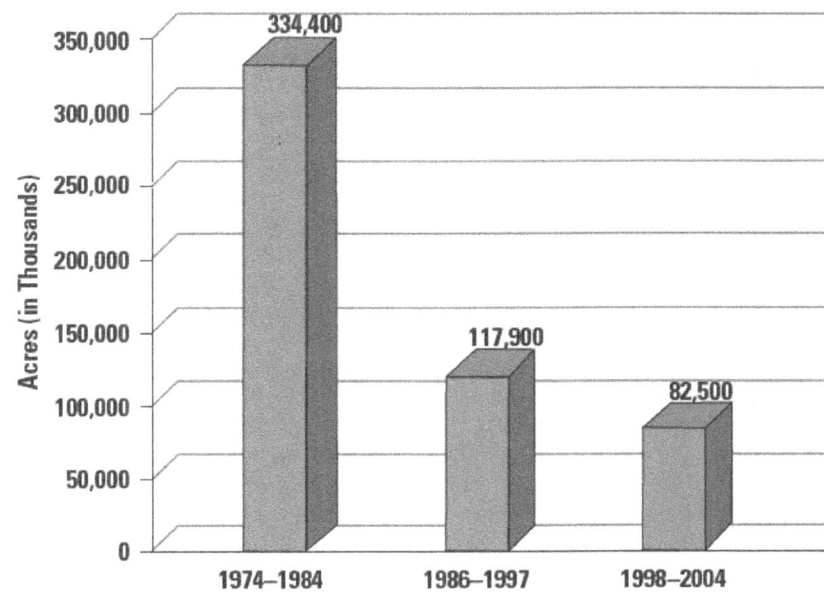

Figure 48. Trends in the estimated annual loss rate of freshwater vegetated wetland area, 1974 to 2004. Sources: Dahl and Johnson 1991; Dahl 2000; and this study.

Figure 49. A mitigation banking site. As wetlands were converted elsewhere, cells of the mitigation bank were flooded to create replacement wetland. 2004.

Freshwater Forested and Shrub Wetlands

Of the estimated 102.5 million acres (41.5 million ha) of freshwater wetlands, 51 percent were forested wetland (over 52 million acres or 21.1 million ha).

Freshwater forested wetlands were affected by two processes, the conversion of forested wetland to and from other wetland types through cutting or the maturation of trees, and loss of forested wetland where wetland hydrology was destroyed.

Freshwater forested wetland area increased between 1998 and 2004 as forested wetlands gained (Table 6) an estimated 548,200 acres (221,950 ha) due to the maturation of wetland shrubs to forests.[10] None of these gains directly resulted from change in any upland category as all of the net gains of forested wetlands came from the wetland shrub category due to succession. Over 1.15 million acres of shrub wetlands had matured and were reclassified as forested wetland.

Estimated net losses of forested wetland to uplands totaled 299,200 acres (121,130 ha). These losses

---

[10] Cowardin *et al.* (1979) required tree height 20 feet (6 meters) or greater to have been classified forested wetland.

of forested wetland to the various upland land uses resulted from the destruction of wetland hydrology and are shown in Figure 50.

Another 63,000 acres (25,500 ha) of forested wetland (Figure 51) were converted to open water ponds. Some of these changes were due to beaver building dams and flooding surrounding timber. An additional 26,600 acres (10,770 ha) became deepwater lakes.

In 2004, an estimated 17.6 million acres (7.1 million ha) of freshwater wetlands were dominated by shrub species or wetland tree species less than 20 feet tall (6 m). Shrub wetlands experienced the largest

change of any vegetated freshwater wetland type. An estimated 900,800 acres (364,700 ha), net were converted to other wetland types between 1998 and 2004. Although wetlands dominated by true shrub species were not uncommon (Figure 52), acreage trends of wetland shrubs were governed primarily by changes in tree species moving to and from forested and shrub categories. During this study, 2.6 million acres (1.05 million ha) of shrub wetlands were converted to forested wetlands (gross). This was very similar to the previous era when 2.4 million acres (972,000 ha) of shrubs were converted to forested wetland.

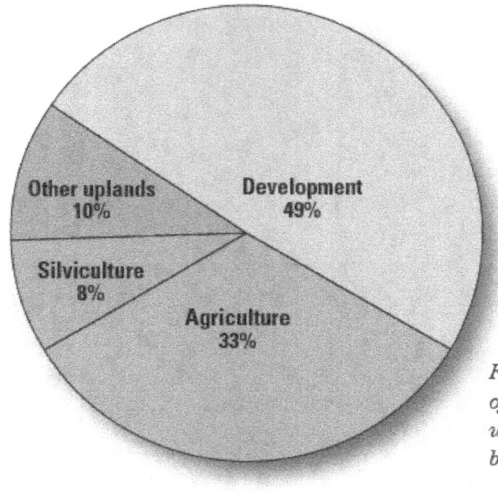

Figure 50. Estimated percent loss of forested wetlands to the various upland land use categories between 1998 and 2004.

Figure 51. Forested wetland. Alabama, 2005. Photo courtesy of South Dakota State University.

An additional 1.4 million acres (567,000 ha) were converted from forested wetlands to shrub wetlands primarily as a result of silviculture. Another 1.04 million acres (406,500 ha) changed from shrub wetland to freshwater emergent wetland. These large shifts between the freshwater categories followed the same magnitude of change as reported between 1986 and 1997.

Long term trends in freshwater forested and shrub wetlands reversed directions (Figure 53). Forested wetland increased for the first time while shrub wetlands declined for the first time since the 1950s.

Figure 52. A freshwater wetland dominated by the woody shrub False Indigo (Amorpha fruticosa). Shrub wetlands contained true shrub species or small tree species under 20 feet (6 meters). Nebraska, 2005.

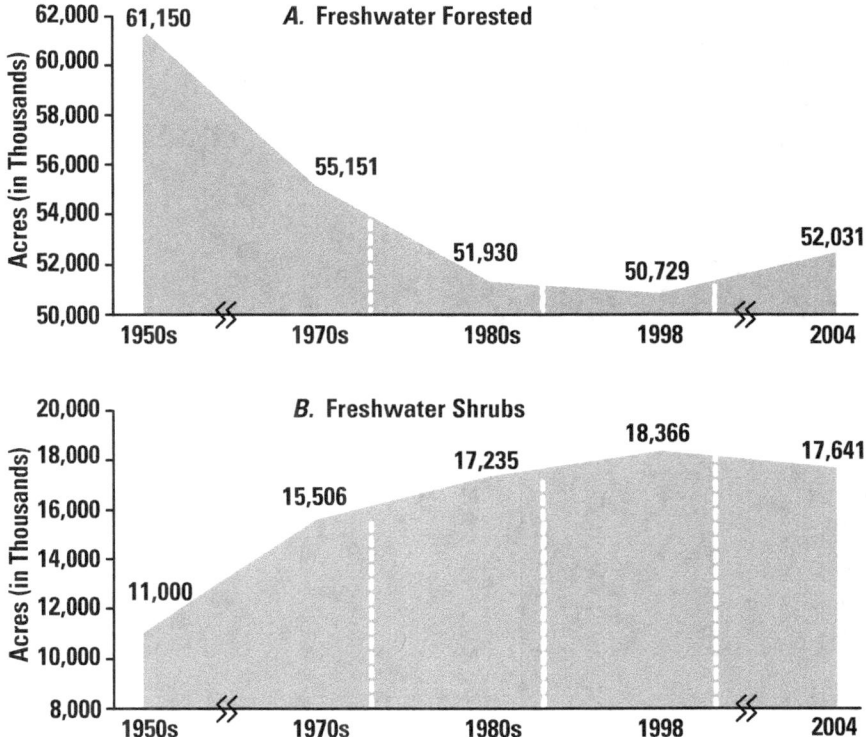

Figure 53. Long-term trends in freshwater forested and shrub wetlands, 1950s to 2004.

Freshwater Emergent Wetlands

In 2004 there were an estimated 26,147,000 acres (10,586,000 ha) of freshwater emergent wetlands. Emergent wetlands declined (Table 5) by an estimated 142,570 acres (57,720 ha). Despite these losses, this represented an 80 percent reduction in the rate of freshwater emergent loss from 1986 to 1997. The "Swampbuster" provisions of the Food Security Act and agricultural set-aside and land retirement programs played an important role in the reduction in emergent wetland losses.

Approximately 83,400 acres of freshwater emergent wetland were lost to upland. An estimated 75 percent of those losses were attributed to agricultural drainage (Figure 54), 17 percent to development and 8 percent to silviculture. This was overshadowed by substantial gains from upland "other" lands (including agriculture in retirement or conservation programs as discussed earlier).

Of the emergent wetlands converted to agriculture, most were small. The average size of emergent wetland converted to agriculture was 4.0 acres (1.6 ha). Many of the conversions were the result of field "round outs" or more thorough drainage of areas that had been only partially drained (Figure 55 A and B). Similar practices such as improvement of on-farm drainage, or elimination of partially drained wetlands permitted under the various Food Security Act revisions were also observed between 1986 and 1997 (Dahl 2000).

Because most freshwater emergent wetlands can reestablish quickly under wet conditions, there is substantial opportunity for restoration. See the insert on *"Restoring Iowa's Prairie Wetlands."*

Long term trends for freshwater emergent wetlands are shown in Figure 56 Freshwater emergent wetlands continue to decline over time.

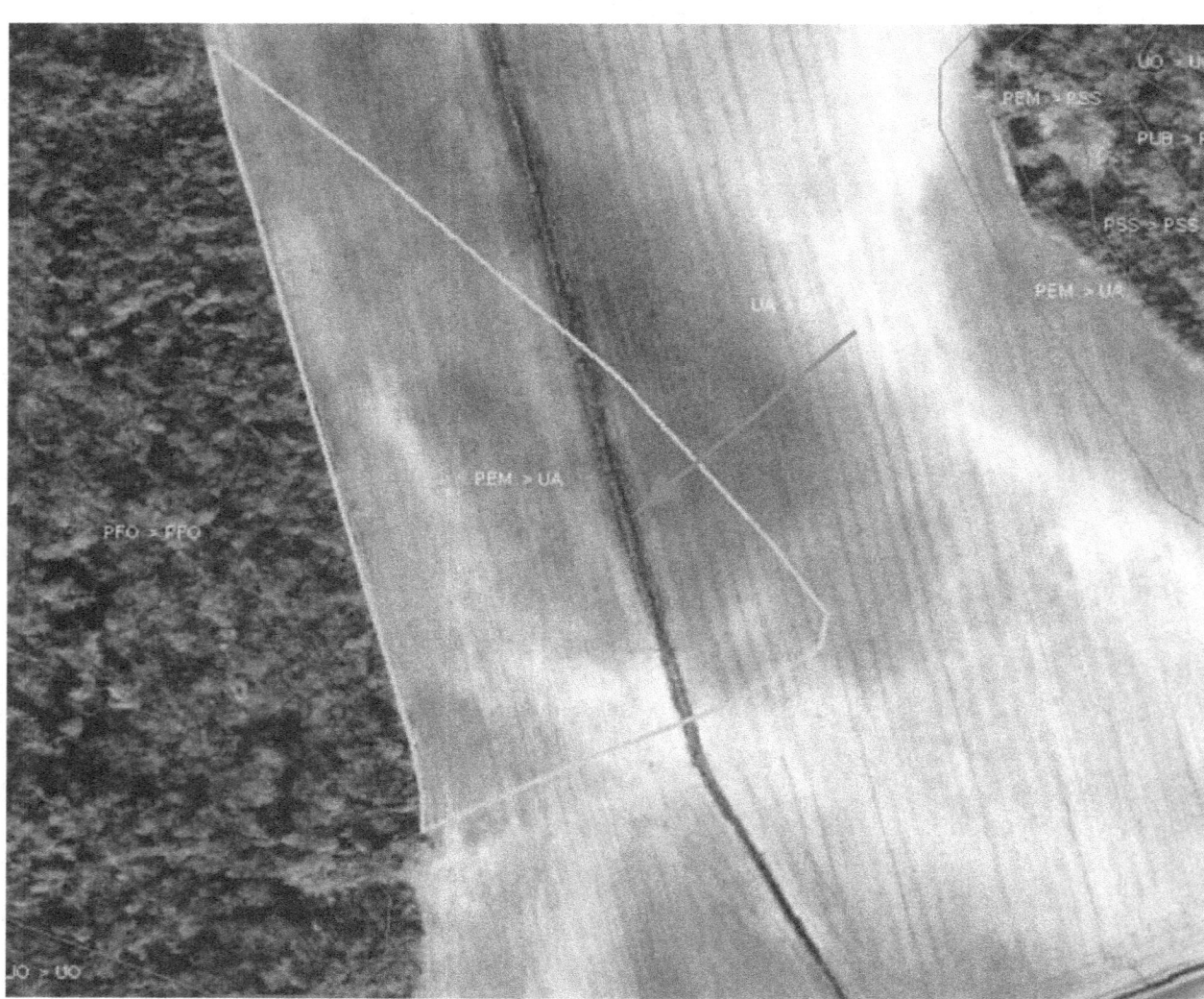

Figure 54. This field has been squared off by agricultural drainage (surface ditch indicated with red arrow). New Jersey, 2003.

A

B

Figure 55 A and B. Subtle wetland drainage practices in the prairie pothole region of South Dakota. Shallow ditches are plowed to facilitate drainage, 2005. Photo courtesy of South Dakota State University.

Figure 56. Long-term trends in freshwater emergent wetlands, 1954 to 2004.

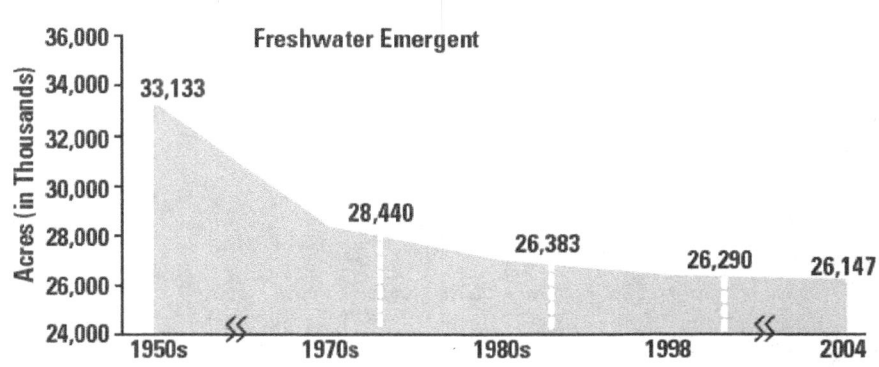

Freshwater ponds

Freshwater ponds were open water areas less than 20 acres (8.1 ha) in size. Ponds were characterized as small bodies of water shallow enough for sunlight to reach the bottom, permitting growth of aquatic plants (Figure 57). Ponds were considered part of the freshwater environment and natural ponds were notable for their abundant and rich varieties of plant and animal life (Lewis 2005).

In this study, ponds were numerous and found throughout the conterminous United States[11]. There were an estimated 6,229,600 acres (2,522,100 ha) of ponds in 2004 (Table 5). Freshwater pond acreage increased 695,400 acres (281,500 ha)

from 1998 to 2004, an 12.6 percent increase (Figure 58). This was the largest percent increase in area of any wetland type in this study.

Without the increased pond acreage, wetland gains would have failed to surpass losses during the timeframe of this study. The creation of artificial freshwater ponds has played a major role in achieving the national wetland quantity objective (Figure 59). Scientists have inferred linkages between wetland structure and function (Mitsch and Gosselink 1993; National Research Council 1995; Brinson and Rheinhardt 1996). Changing the abundance of wetland types (vegetated wetland to open water wetland), also changes wetland structure and can affect other ecological characteristics.

Kentula *et al.* (1993) found that ponds with a fringe of emergent marsh composed the majority of compensatory mitigation projects required nationally under Section 404 of the Clean Water Act. Open water ponds were

created as mitigation for a variety of types of wetlands in Oregon, California, Washington and several southeastern states (Gwin *et al.* 1999).

Some open water ponds might eventually become vegetated wetlands through successional changes or through re-establishment of vegetation. However, only two percent of created ponds from the 1986 to 1997 study (Dahl 2000) were reclassified as vegetated wetlands in this study. This indicated ponds had either been designed and maintained as open water basins (water retention, ornamentation) or projects intended to provide vegetated wetlands as a means of restoration and creation lacked vegetation after several years.

Cowardin *et al.* (1979) recognized ponds as an important component of the aquatic ecosystem and included them within a larger system of freshwater wetlands. Classical limnology recognized five distinct types of ponds: Cypress ponds,

---

[11] One of the most important objectives of this study was to monitor gains and losses of all wetland areas. The concept that certain kinds of wetlands with certain functions (e.g., human-constructed ponds on a golf course) should have been excluded was rejected. To discriminate on the basis of qualitative considerations would have required a much larger and more intensive qualitative assessment. The data presented do not address functional replacement with loss or gain of wetland area.

Figure 57. A freshwater pond in central Kansas is starting to support emergent vegetation, 2005.

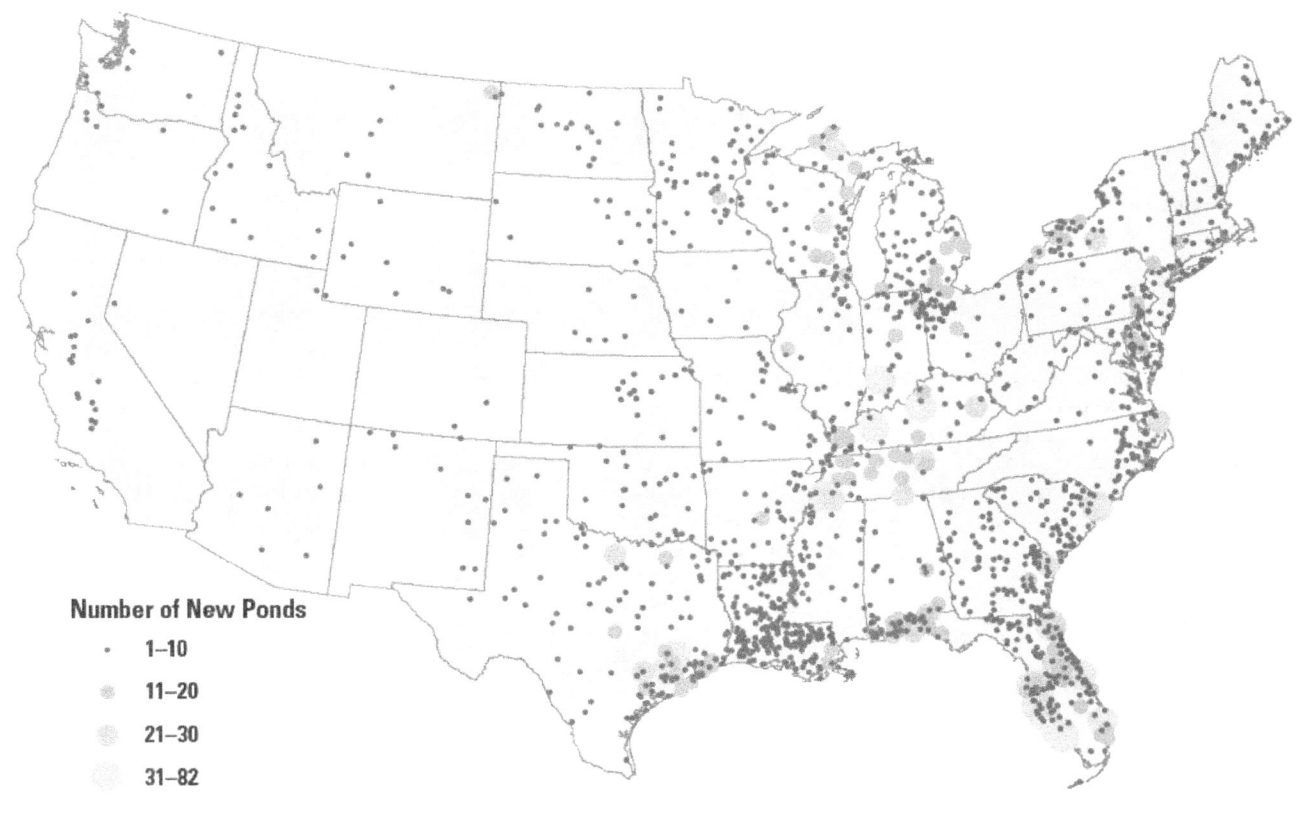

Number of New Ponds

- · 1–10
- ○ 11–20
- ○ 21–30
- ○ 31–82

Figure 58. Number and approximate location of new freshwater ponds created between 1998 and 2004.

Figure 59. A newly created open water pond as part of a golf course. Maryland, 2005.

bog ponds, meadow-stream ponds, mountain ponds and man-made farm ponds (Lewis 2005). With the exception of the last type, none of the created ponds found during this study met these descriptions. Most of the ponds that were created were of the kind discussed below.

The creation of freshwater fishing ponds has been very popular in many states. Bass (*Micropterus spp.*) and bluegill[12] have been widely introduced for sport fishing into small warm water lakes and ponds. Pond construction and fish stocking has steadily grown in popularity so that bass-bluegill form the foundation of warm water sport

---

[12] Includes numerous species of the family Centrarchidae known by various common names such as sunfish, pumpkinseed, redear, longear, rock bass, green sunfish and others.

fishing in ponds and small bodies of water (Ney and Helfrich 2003). These fishing ponds form a portion of the newly created ponds that were added to the wetlands acreage base.

The creation of artificial water detention, retention and water hazard ponds has also contributed to the number of ponds designed and used solely for ornamentation or water management. In many cases these have been constructed to provide a single function—the collection of runoff and water control. Water quality and aesthetics were of little importance (Beaulieu 2005), and plant growth was controlled or regularly eliminated. These ponds are not an equivalent replacement for vegetated wetlands (Dahl 2000). Figure 60 A–D shows some of the created ponds found during this study.

Ponds for aesthetics or water management have been incorporated into many residential and commercial developments (Figure 61).

Aquaculture has also contributed to artificial pond construction. Aquaculture production consisted of fish for food, ornamental fish, baitfish, mollusks, crustaceans, aquatic plants (Figure 62), algae and some reptiles such as alligators and turtles. In the 1990s the value of United States aquaculture production rose over 400 percent. The catfish industry was the largest sector, concentrated in Mississippi, Alabama, Arkansas and Louisiana (USDA—ERS 2005).

The long-term trends in freshwater ponds are shown in Figure 63. Freshwater pond area has continued to increase over time.

A Nebraska, 2005

C Wisconsin, 2005

B Indiana, 2005

D Iowa, 2004

Figure 60 A–D. Different ponds have been constructed for different purposes throughout the United States.

Figure 61. Color infrared aerial photograph of new development in south Florida. Ponds and small residential lakes (shown as dark blue) are surrounded by new housing.

Figure 62. Commercial cranberry operations in Wisconsin had created several open water ponds (dark blue areas). Water was used to flood cranberry plants grown in the rectangular basins (red). Ikonos imagery, 2005, courtesy of Space Imaging Corp.

Figure 63. Long-term trends in freshwater pond acreage, 1954 to 2004.

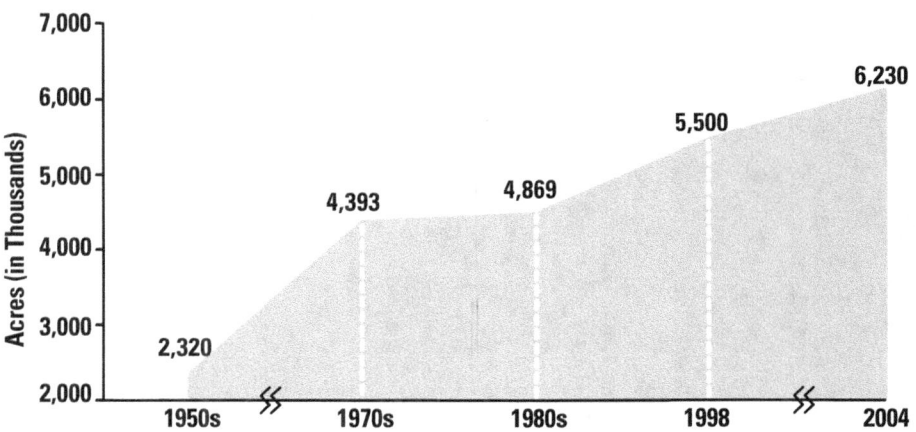

Freshwater Lakes and Reservoirs

Lakes were most prevalent in Minnesota, Wisconsin, Michigan and Florida. These water bodies were often associated with fringes of wetland vegetation. They supported inland fisheries and waterfowl and have been very important to people as sites for recreation (Figure 64).

Deepwater lakes and reservoirs showed an increase, with a net gain of 162,900 acres (66,000 ha). The rate of increase was much less than 30 to 40 years ago when large reservoirs were being built. Dahl (2000) reported that lake and reservoir creation declined 43 percent in recent decades. That trend held for this study. The freshwater lakes created during the study period were associated with urban developments.

A Indiana, 2005

B Wisconsin, 2005

Figure 64 A and B. Freshwater lakes provide wildlife and fish habitat as well as opportunities for recreation and education.

Terminology and Tracking Wetland Gains

In the past, Federal agencies have used inconsistent terminology to describe human actions taken to increase wetland area or improve wetland condition. For example, "restoration" has often been used to describe the return of hydrology and wetland vegetation to a former wetland, and also to describe actions taken to manage function, or the enhancement of condition. The Council on Environmental Quality's report Conserving America's Wetlands (CEQ 2005) attempted to clarify some of the ambiguity by providing definitions for "restore," "create," "improve" and "protect" wetlands (Figures 65 through 68).

In December, 2004 CEQ assembled information related to wetland actions taken by federal agencies to meet the Administration's wetland goal of achieving an "overall increase" in the quantity and quality of wetlands by restoring, improving and protecting more than 3 million acres (1.2 million ha) in five years (CEQ 2005). That report provided information on wetland area and functional gains made or planned by federal agencies. It did not report gains or losses made or planned by other agencies or by individuals, corporations, conservation groups or other non-federal entities.

This report differs from the CEQ report in the following ways: Wetland restoration as used in this study refers only to restoration of previously drained, diked or filled wetland area and makes no attempt to determine wetland function or distinguish between wetlands of different quality. Consequently, wetland "improvement" and wetland "protection" were not measured as part of this study because they do not result in wetland area gains. Most notably this study determined statistical estimates of wetland losses between 1998 and 2004 as

Figure 65. Created wetland on an area that was upland (dry land). This definition is the same for both the federal agency wetland gains reporting and this study. Central Wisconsin, 2005.

Figure 66. A wetland restoration (re-establishment). This former wetland basin had been completely drained and reclassified as upland. Photo courtesy of South Dakota State University.

Figure 67. "Improved" wetland or wetland enhancement—hydrology has been restored to an existing albeit degraded wetland. This rehabilitation improved wetland value(s), but these types of changes resulted in no change in wetland acreage and were not included as change areas in this study. NRCS Wetland Reserve, Nebraska, 2005.

Figure 68. Wetland Protection or preservation included pre-existing wetland acres either owned or leased long-term by a federal agency. Since this action resulted in no change in wetland area it did not reflect a change as part of this study. Federal (USFWS) Waterfowl Production Area.

well as all wetland gains, including those undertaken by state, local and private entities. Table 6 contrasts other features between this report and the 2005 CEQ report on wetland gains.

The Council on Environmental Quality (2005) reported that Federal agencies had collectively restored or created 328,000 acres (132,800 ha) of wetlands between 2004 and 2005.

When contrasting the results of this study with Conserving America's Wetlands (CEQ 2005) report on wetland gains, the two studies used different methods and provided different results. This study included wetland losses as well as wetland gains. This study also measured wetland change between 1998 and 2004, whereas CEQ considered only changes from 2004 and 2005.

Table 6. Contrasting the Fish and Wildlife Service's Wetlands Status and Trends with the Council on Environmental Quality report (2005) on federal efforts to track wetland gains.

Reporting Element	Wetlands Status and Trends (FWS)	Conserving America's Wetlands (2005)
Timeframe	Changes observed between 1998 and 2004	2004 and projected 2005 performance information
Measure (acres)	Scientifically based statistical sampling of actual change observed on 4,682 4-square mile sample plots	Administrative accounting of reported and projected gains due to federal activities
Reported Change	Statistical estimates of wetland gains, losses, and net change	Wetland gains as defined by study
Type of Change	Acreage change(s) only (gains and losses) with statistical error rate	Wetland creation (acres), wetlands improvement (acres or function), and wetland protection
Wetland Descriptors	Identifies extent by 16 wetland and deepwater habitat types (i.e. vegetated wetland types can be distinguished from ponds)	Single general "wetland" category (i.e. ponds are not distinguished from other wetland types)
Study Area	Conterminous United States	Entire United States
Interagency Cooperation	Yes, included Council on Environmental Quality, Office of Management and Budget, Dept. of Agriculture, Dept. of Interior, Army Corps of Engineers, Dept. of Transportation, Environmental Protection Agency, National Oceanic and Atmospheric Administration, state resource agencies and non-governmental organizations	Yes, included Council on Environmental Quality, Office of Management and Budget, Dept. of Agriculture, Dept. of Interior, Army Corps of Engineers, Dept. of Transportation, Environmental Protection Agency, National Oceanic and Atmospheric Administration
Peer Review	Reviewed by principal federal agencies as well as independent expert peer review	Review by federal agencies contributing data
Field Component	Field verification of 32 percent of the sample data sites	No field component

Wetland Restoration and Creation on Conservation Lands

Federal policies and programs during the past decade have increasingly emphasized wetland restoration (Zinn and Copeland 2002), both on public lands and on lands in private ownership. The federal land management agencies have been much more than facilitators of wetland restoration and creation; they have restored wetlands on federal properties, including National Parks and Preserves, National Wildlife Refuges, National Forests and lands managed by the Bureau of Land Management (Figure 69). A representative listing of the wetland restoration programs and activities is shown in Appendix D.

Many National Wildlife Refuges provide opportunities for wetland restoration, creation or enhancement. The Refuge System has maintained active programs to reestablish wetlands within refuge boundaries (CEQ 2005). An example of collaborative wetland restoration work along the Upper Mississippi River is highlighted in the following insert.

Figure 69. A system of federal lands including National Wildlife Refuges and Wetland Management Districts are restoring and enhancing wetland acres.

Wetland Restoration on the Upper Mississippi River National Wildlife and Fish Refuge

The Upper Mississippi River National Wildlife and Fish Refuge was created in 1924 largely through the efforts of the Izaak Walton League in an effort to protect habitat for black bass. Unlike most refuges, Congress established the Upper Mississippi River National Wildlife and Fish Refuge for both fish and wildlife. It became the only refuge in the nation designated as a wildlife and fish refuge.

The Refuge consists of almost 240,000 acres (97,200 ha) of wooded islands, bottomland forests, backwater sloughs, bays and marshes. It represents one of the largest contiguous stretches of wetland and aquatic habitats in the Midwestern part of the United States. The Refuge extends along the Mississippi River 261 miles from Wabasha, Minnesota to Rock Island, Illinois.

Wetlands and other waters of the Refuge support about 5,000 great blue heron (*Ardea herodias*) nests in 15 colonies, 50 percent of the continent's canvasback duck (*Aythya valisineria*) population and 20 percent of the continent's tundra swans (*Cygnus columbianus*) during their respective fall migrations. Other species of ducks on the Refuge include lesser scaup (*Aythya affinis*), ring necked duck (*Aythya collaris*), American wigeon (*Anas americana*), mallard (*Anas platyrhnchos*), wood duck (*Aix sponsa*), and common merganser (*Mergus merganser*). There are over 100 known bald eagle nests and the river is home to 134 fish species including important sport fish such as walleye (*Sander vitreus*), largemouth and smallmouth bass (*Micropterus spp.*), channel catfish (*Ictalurus punctatus*), northern pike (*Esox lucius*), bluegill (*Lepomis spp.*) and black crappies (*Pomoxis nigromaculatus*).

When the river was impounded, water levels were permanently raised and greatly changed the character of the river and its associated habitats. Since the time of impoundment, sediment accumulation, long term inundation, and erosion have contributed to a process where wetlands and backwaters lose their vegetation and are converted to open water. This process has decreased habitat for plants and animals and important wetland habitats have disappeared.

The Environmental Management Program is a coordinated habitat restoration program for the upper Mississippi River. It is administered by the Army Corps of Engineers in partnership with the Fish and Wildlife Service and several other federal, state and non-governmental organizations. The purpose is to implement habitat restoration projects that will counteract the effects of an aging impounded river system by changing the river's floodplain structure and hydrology. Since its inception, the program has restored and improved 105,000 acres (43,500 ha) along the upper Mississippi River corridor.

The Stoddard Islands Restoration Project was one of the efforts completed on the Refuge under the Environmental Management Program in 1999. The project was located in Pool 8 adjacent to Stoddard, Wisconsin (near La Crosse, Wisconsin) and was designed to restore acres of wetlands that had washed away and improve related habitats in Stoddard Bay.

The project incorporated backwater dredging, island construction, and bank stabilization to restore and improve 500 acres (200 ha). Seven islands were constructed from dredge material to reduce current flows and water turbidity that had destroyed aquatic plant beds in the backwaters. The dredged material had a dual purpose: it created deep pools for overwintering fish habitat and subsequently was used to create earthen islands as wind breaks that promoted the growth of aquatic vegetation. Rock sills allowed waters into the area during periods of high flow. A notch in the sill was designed to limit flows during low flow periods. The rehabilitation work created habitat diversity and was designed to support a range of vegetation types.

Once the project was completed, subsequent monitoring of the site indicated increased use by ducks and swans, sport fish and other wetland dependent species.

Oblique view of some of the numerous wetlands and islands that form the Upper Mississippi River National Wildlife and Fish Refuge. Photo courtesy of Robert Hurt.

1994

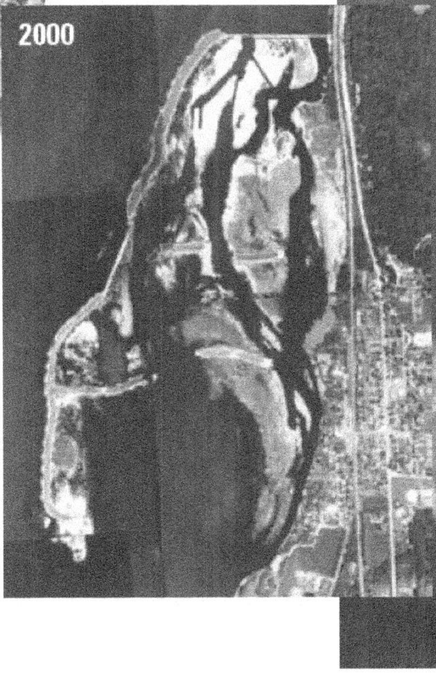

2000

Stoddard Islands Restoration Project before restoration of habitats (1994) and after (2000). About 500 acres (200 ha) were restored.

Historically, many areas of the United States had experienced wetland losses due to agricultural development. These areas have the potential to restore wetlands through various programs and initiatives. Iowa is one such example. Historical wetland losses in Iowa's prairie pothole region exceeded 90 percent (Dahl 1990 b). These pothole wetlands are generally small, topographic depressions, dominated by emergent marsh vegetation and can be easily restored.

Prairie pothole wetland.Photo courtesy of the FWS.

Restoring Iowa's Prairie Marshes

Located in the southern and easternmost portion of the Prairie Pothole Region (PPR), North Central Iowa once supported a complex of temporary and seasonal wetlands amid many large, deepwater marshes and shallow lakes. Iowa historically received the most consistent annual rainfall of any portion of the PPR. This environment, with its long growing season and deep, rich soils, provides some of the most productive agricultural lands in the world.

Agriculture converted many of Iowa's prairie wetlands. Much of the conversion took place in the early 1900s and most of the wetlands had been drained by 1920. Organized drainage districts were formed to provide a network of shared tile mains and ditches. When this system was built, individual landowners had an outlet for their own private drainage systems.

The conversion of wetlands to farmland through a network of underground pipes is a marvel of both engineering and sheer determination. Most of the Iowa PPR still relies on drainage provided by the "shared infrastructure" that is nearly a century old. Over this same time period, thousands of miles of private tile have been replaced or installed. This system of wetland drainage has resulted in the loss of 95 to 98 percent of the prairie pothole wetlands in Iowa.

Although the conversion of natural habitats to agricultural production in Iowa is extensive, implementation of the Food Security Act of 1985

Historical extent of the Prairie Pothole Region of North America

Installation of subsurface tile for wetland drainage in Iowa, circa 1950. Photo courtesy of USFWS.

and development of the North America Waterfowl Management Plan (NAWMP) in 1987 marked a turning point. Fish and Wildlife Service and U.S. Department of Agriculture programs combined to provide funds to restore wetlands and integrate natural habitats into the agricultural landscape. In Iowa, federal funds have stimulated a substantial commitment of resources from state and local governments, conservation organizations, and other partners to cooperatively implement successful wetland restoration programs in the most intensively drained part of the PPR and to reverse the trend of continued habitat loss. About 61,185 acres (24,770 ha) have been acquired since 1987 by public agencies for conservation and restoration of native vegetation communities, management of wildlife populations, and to provide outdoor recreation opportunities. Through acquisition of these lands, Iowa has protected 4,562 acres (1,850 ha) of existing wetlands. On other public lands 1,576 wetland basins totaling 8,718

This photograph shows crop loss in a drained, farmed wetland. Most pothole wetlands have been drained with sub-surface tile rather than ditched (surface drained) or filled. Their footprints are still very visible on the landscape and restoration can be accomplished relatively simply. Photo courtesy of Iowa DNR.

Aerial view of Union Hills Waterfowl Production Area, Iowa —an example of a successful wetland complex restoration. Photo courtesy of Iowa DNR.

acres (3,530 ha) have been restored. These acquisitions include more than 44,000 acres (17,800 ha) of uplands, the majority seeded to grasslands.

Restoration of wetlands and associated uplands from row crops to grasslands is essential to the long-term conservation of wetland habitats and wildlife, especially upland nesting waterfowl and other water birds. These upland habitats also support an array of grassland birds, many of which are of special concern due to long-term population declines.

Agricultural conservation programs have also been crucial to reestablishing wetland-grassland complexes. Currently, active Conservation Reserve Program (CRP) contracts for wetlands cover 77,574 acres (31,400 ha) across the Iowa PPR. Estimated wetland acres total 22,580 (9,140 ha) with 54,994 acres (22.265 ha) of wetlands-associated grasslands seeded as wetland buffers. An additional 31,095 acres (12,590 ha) of upland and wetland have been protected under the Wetland Reserve Program easements on private land. The vast majority of these easements are perpetual, resulting in permanent protection for approximately 7,500 wetland acres (3,040 ha). These results do not include other CRP practices that provide additional wildlife habitats, especially grasslands. Many of these grassland acres are in the proximity of wetlands and provide nesting habitats for waterfowl and other upland-nesting migratory birds.

Iowa has successfully built wetland-grassland complexes by focusing wetland restoration programs on 101 priority areas that range from 1 to 59 square miles (2.6

to 152.8 sq km). No single program can achieve the results desired for the PPR wetland complexes. The success depends on a coordinated program for both public and private lands. Land acquisition to establish long-term protection and active management in combination with perpetual easements and short term contracts on private lands will achieve the landscape-level habitat goals.

Through planning, patience and partnerships, wetlands are becoming more common and appreciated in North-Central Iowa's agricultural landscape.

Bordered on the east by the Mississippi River and on the west by the Missouri River, Iowa is centrally located along one of the most important migration routes in North America. The value of these wetlands during

Wetland Reserve acres in central Iowa, 2005.

migration, particularly in spring, has received more attention. Continued increases in wetland quality and quantity in Iowa would benefit the breeding success of birds across a much larger geographic area.

In Iowa it has become very important for rural and urban communities to observe how agriculture and wetlands can co-exist to benefit people. Wetland restoration activities have gained acceptance from Iowans, both economically and environmentally, and there is great potential to continue to restore wetlands and grasslands throughout Iowa.

Todd Bishop
Special Projects Coordinator, Wildlife Bureau
Iowa Department of Natural Resources

Map showing the footprints of drained wetland basins (blue) in the Prairie Pothole Region of Iowa. The potential for wetland restoration remains high. Image courtesy of the Iowa DNR.

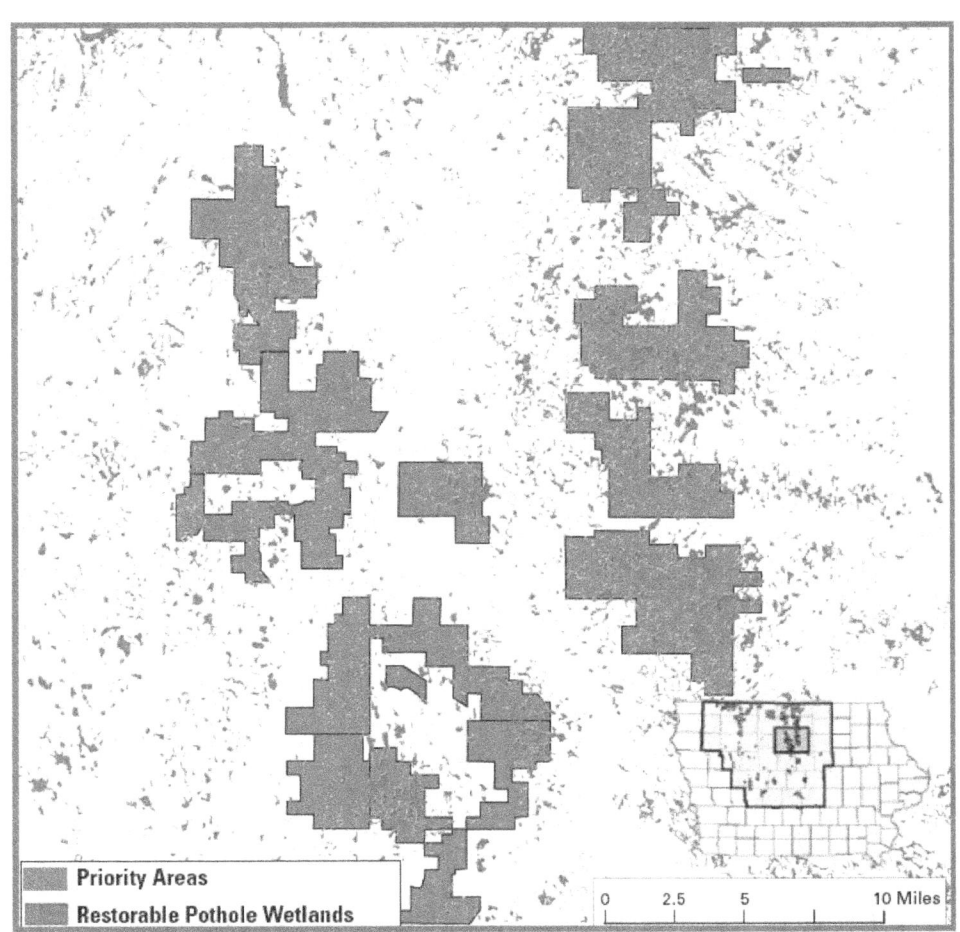

A diversity of bird species including shorebirds and water birds migrate through Iowa and use wetland habitats for resting and feeding.

Iowa prairie pothole wetland.

Common moorhen (*Gallinula chloropus*). Photo by Jim Rathert.

Long-billed dowitcher (*Limnodromus scolopaceus*). Photo by Lee Karney.

Lesser scaup (*Aythya affinis*). Photo by Dave Menke.

Canada geese (*Branta canadensis*). Photo by Glen Smart.

Bufflehead (*Bucephala albeola*) and greater scaup (*Aythya marila*). Photo by Donna Dewhurst.

Wood duck (*Aix sponsa*) pair, male in front, female in back. Photo by Dave Menke.

Monitoring Wetland Quantity and Quality—Beyond No-Net-Loss

As noted earlier, this study tracked changes in wetland area and type (classification) and the causes of those changes with respect to land use (e.g., loss to urban development). Changes in wetland quality (function and condition) were not included.

Monitoring wetland quality poses special challenges. Some states have already started to plan for this endeavor through the development of comprehensive studies to address both wetland quantity and quality. Minnesota has provided one example of the process now being undertaken.[13]

---

[13] See the insert section on "**Minnesota's Comprehensive Wetlands Monitoring Plan.**"

Bald eagles (Haliaeetus leucocephalus) occupy a bald cypress tree at Reelfoot National Wildlife Refuge, Tennessee. Photo by David Haggard.

Minnesota's Comprehensive Wetland Assessment and Monitoring Strategy

Minnesota, land of 10,000 lakes, is home to over 10 million acres of wetlands. Minnesota remains a wetland rich state, although the current wetland extent is about half of what was present before European settlement (Dahl 1990). Encouraged by government policies and subsidies in place until the early 1970s, landowners drained much of Minnesota to grow crops. Wetland loss was particularly acute in the prairie regions of the state, where more than 90 percent of the original wetlands have been drained. Although wetland drainage produced rich farmland and brought economic prosperity to the region, it has also had profound effects on water quality, fish and wildlife habitat, flooding frequency and recreational opportunities.

Reflecting growing public appreciation of the value of the remaining wetlands, the Minnesota Wetland Conservation Act (WCA) was enacted in 1991. The Act established state policy to:

- achieve no net loss in the quantity, quality, and biological diversity of Minnesota's existing wetlands and

- increase the quantity, quality, and biological diversity of Minnesota's wetlands by restoring or enhancing degraded or drained wetlands.

Due to actions resulting from the WCA and other state and federal programs, particularly the Swampbuster provisions of the Farm Bill, the rate of wetland loss has declined substantially. Tens of thousands of wetland acres have been restored or enhanced under state and federal voluntary conservation programs. To know if the state's wetland goals are being achieved, accurate accounting and current state specific status information is needed.

As a first step toward addressing this problem, a group of Minnesota state agencies involved in wetland regulation and management (Pollution Control Agency, Department

of Natural Resources, Board of Water and Soil Resources) applied for and received a USEPA State Wetlands Program Development Grant to develop a comprehensive wetland assessment, monitoring and mapping strategy. The objectives of this strategy are to provide an accurate, ongoing assessment of the statewide status and trends in wetland quantity and quality and to relate the observed changes to programmatic actions.

Work on the strategy began in 2003 and the development effort is structured to include staff representation from the Pollution Control Agency, with assistance provided

A wetland mitigation project, Minnesota, 2005.

by the Department of Natural Resources and Board of Water and Soil Resources. A consortium of state and federal biologists, managers and stakeholders form the project's technical and oversight teams.

Although Minnesota's wetland assessment and monitoring strategy is not yet fully developed, it is clear that many approaches will be needed to meet the project's objectives. The following key components have been identified:

Stratified random sampling using remote imagery —This component of the monitoring and assessment strategy is an intensification of the Fish and Wildlife Service's status and trends effort for detecting changes in wetland quantity. Current tasks involve determining the number and distribution of plots necessary to obtain an accurate assessment of wetland gain and loss over time. Because wetlands are not uniformly distributed across the state, one task is how to best stratify the sampling design to enhance reporting accuracy within specified geographic areas.

Updating Wetland maps—Although the sampling component will be useful in detecting trends over time, the best method for obtaining an accurate assessment of the current status of wetlands is through a mapping effort. Hence, the strategy calls for using Fish and Wildlife Service protocols to develop updated wetland maps for the state. Due to the expense of this component ($6–7 million for the state), the update would likely be done in phases over several years. In rapidly developing areas and in parts of the state where restoration programs are most active, periodic updates of the maps will complement the random sampling component in assessing gains and losses.

Wetland quality assessment—Several methods for assessing wetland quality status and trends are being explored. These include landscape assessments, such as the Landscape Development Index (Brown and Vivas 2005) and site-specific methods as Indexes of Biological Integrity (plant and invertebrate IBIs have already been developed for depressional wetlands in Minnesota), and functional value assessments as the Minnesota Routine Assessment Method. It is likely that the final strategy will identify a mix of wetland quality assessment protocols and will probably utilize the random sampling plots described above.

Integrated wetland database—One reason for Minnesota's current inability to accurately report net wetland gain/loss is that there are so many agencies and groups involved in wetland regulation and restoration and there is no coordination among their various project tracking systems. For example, a particular wetland

impact may be regulated under the state WCA and by the Corps of Engineers under the Section 404 program. Hence, when compiling agency accomplishment reports, the same impact may be counted twice. A similar situation occurs for wetland restorations having multiple partners. The assessment and monitoring strategy also calls for developing an integrated wetland project database that will import project data from various agency and program tracking systems. The database will be geo-referenced, so that a proposed gain or loss shows as a single project, even if reported by more than one agency. The accumulated data in the database will complement the random sampling component in assessing overall wetland trends and will help relate the observed changes to various programs, providing a basis for assessing program effectiveness. As an initial step, the Board of Water and Soil Resources received a USEPA grant to develop an electronic wetland permitting/tracking system that would facilitate the capture of wetland project data. Complete development of an integrated wetland database will be a challenge, but is an important component of the comprehensive monitoring and assessment strategy.

The assessment and monitoring strategy is scheduled to be completed by January 2006. Permanent, partial funding for implementation of the strategy is included in the state budget starting in fiscal year 2006. In addition, the USEPA recently awarded Minnesota a Wetland Demonstration Program Grant to provide additional start-up funding for three years. Work is anticipated to being on the random sampling component and some wetland mapping in the spring of 2006.

Doug Norris
Wetlands Program Coordinator
Minnesota Department of Natural Resources
Ecological Services Division, St. Paul, MN

Mark Gernes
Minnesota Pollution Control Agency
St. Paul, MN

Summary

Cypress and other wetland vegetation fringe the edge of a lake.

This study measured trends in wetland acreage in the conterminous United States between 1998 and 2004. The Cowardin *et al.* (1979) wetland definition was used to describe wetland types. Wetland trends were measured through the acquisition and analysis of contemporary remotely sensed imagery for 4,682 randomly selected sample plots throughout the conterminous United States. Field verification was completed for 32 percent of the sample areas in portions of 35 states. This provided a scientifically grounded analysis of the aerial extent of all wetlands in the lower 48 states, regardless of ownership.

The wetland goals of the United States have traditionally been based on wetland acreage and the ability to provide a quantitative measure of the extent of wetland area to gauge progress toward achieving the national goal of "no-net-loss." This latest study provides scientific and statistical results that led to the conclusion that wetland acreage gains acquired through restoration and creation have outdistanced losses. Between 1998 and 2004 there was a net gain of 191,750 wetland acres (77,630 ha). This equated to an average annual net gain of 32,000 acres (12,900 ha). Factors contributing to this included: Creation of almost 700,000 acres (282,000 ha) of open water ponds, agricultural conservation programs, land set-asides, retirement programs, disincentives for wetland drainage, wetland restoration and creation programs that have involved partners especially on conservation lands, education and awareness about wetland values and functions and, federal and state wetland management programs.

Contributing to the net gain in wetland area was a reduction in the overall rate of human-induced wetland loss. However, vegetated wetlands, particularly estuarine and freshwater emergent wetlands, continued to be destroyed albeit at a reduced rate. These wetlands are important to a number of wildlife species and additional efforts to ensure restoration of these habitats are needed in the future.

This report does not draw conclusions regarding trends in the quality of the nation's wetlands. The Status and Trends Study collects data on wetland acreage gains and losses, as it has for the past 50 years. However, it is timely to examine the quality, function, and condition of such wetland acreage. Such an examination will be undertaken by agencies participating in the President's Wetlands Initiative.

Estuarine and Marine Wetlands

Three major categories of estuarine and marine wetlands were included in this study: estuarine intertidal emergents (salt and brackish water marshes), estuarine shrub wetlands (mangrove swamps or mangles and other salt tolerant woody species) and estuarine and marine intertidal non-vegetated wetlands.

This study estimated that in 2004 there were slightly more than 5.3 million acres (2.1 million ha) of marine and estuarine wetlands in the conterminous United States. Estuarine emergent (salt marsh) made up an estimated 73 percent of all estuarine and marine wetlands. Estuarine shrub wetlands made up 13 percent and non-vegetated saltwater wetlands 14 percent by area.

Estuarine vegetated wetlands declined by an estimated 32,400 acres (13,120 ha) between 1998 and 2004. Estuarine non-vegetated wetlands experienced a net gain of an estimated 4,000 ac (2,390 ha). The overriding factor in the decline of estuarine and marine wetlands was loss of emergent salt marsh to open saltwater systems.

Freshwater Wetlands

An estimated 95 percent of all wetlands were in the freshwater system. Among freshwater wetlands, forested wetlands made up an estimated 51 percent of the total area. Freshwater emergent wetland made up 25.5 percent, shrub wetlands 17 percent and freshwater ponds 6.5 percent by area. Almost all net gains of wetland observed between 1998 and 2004 were in freshwater wetland types.

The estimated area of freshwater forested wetland increased by 548,200 acres (221,950 ha) between 1998 and 2004. These changes resulted from succession from shrub wetlands to forested wetland. Freshwater shrubs and emergent wetlands declined between 1998 and 2004.

Freshwater emergent wetlands declined by an estimated 142,570 acres (57,720 ha), most have been lost to agriculture. Wetland restorations helped ameliorate some wetland losses, but small wetlands or smaller portions of larger wetlands continued to be destroyed. Findings indicated that eighty five percent of all freshwater wetland losses were wetlands less than 5.0 acres (2.0 ha). Fifty two percent were wetlands less than 1.0 acre (0.4 ha).

There was a substantial increase in the number of open water ponds as pond area increased by an estimated 12.6 percent. Without the increased pond acreage, wetland gains would not have surpassed wetland losses during the timeframe of this study. Although increases in pond acreage were important in meeting the national wetland quantity goals, creation of some types of ponds may not meet the wetland quality goals established in 2004. Ponds created as mitigation for the loss of some vegetated wetland types are not an equivalent replacement for those wetlands. Gauging the functional value of ponds and predicting their long term viability will require additional work.

Certain regions of the country experienced larger changes than others. Florida and Louisiana were more prominent in the estimated amount of wetland lost and gained between 1998 and 2004. Other regions undergoing rapid changes (losses or gains) warrant future monitoring of wetland trends. The Fish and Wildlife Service, in fulfillment of the President's 2004 directive, will work with other federal and state partners to complete wetland status and trend reports to address these and other priority areas.

Kootenai National Wildlife Refuge, Idaho. Photo by John and Karen Hollingsworth.

References Cited

Ainslie, W.B. 2002. Forested Wetlands. *In*: Wear, D.N. and J.G. Greis. Southern Forest Resource Assessment. Gen Tech. Rep. SRS-53. U.S. Department of Agriculture, Southern Forest Research Station, Asheville, NC. pp. 479–499.

Aldrich, R.C. 1979. Remote sensing of wildland resources: A state-of-the-art review. USDA Forest Service, General Technical Report RM–71, Rocky Mt. Forest and Range Experiment Station, Ft. Collins, CO. 56 p.

Anderson, J.R., E.E. Hardy, J.T. Roach and R.E. Winter. 1976. A land use and land cover classification system for use with remote sensor data. U.S. Geological Survey Professional Paper 964. U.S. Geological Survey, Washington, D.C. 28 p.Avery, T.E. 1968. *Interpretation of Aerial Photographs* 2nd edition. Burgess Publishing Co., Minneapolis, MN. 324 p.

Beaulier, E. 2005. Ornamental and Retention Ponds. Land and Water. Vol. 49, No. 2. pp. 2–14.

Brinson, M.M. and R. Rheinhardt. 1996. The role of reference wetlands in functional assessment and mitigation. Ecological Applications, 6:69–76.

Brown, M.T. and M.B. Vivas. 2005. Landscape development intensity index. Environmental Monitoring and Assessment. 101:289-309.

Chabreck, R.A. 1988. Coastal Marshes, ecology and wildlife management. University of Minnesota Press, Minneapolis, MN. 138 p.

Coastal America. 2003. Enhancing stewardship of our coastal environment, 2003 Coastal America Progress Report. Washington, D.C. 43 p.

Council on Environmental Quality. 2005. Conserving America's Wetlands Implementing the President's Goal. Executive Office of the President, Washington, D.C. 37 p.

Cowardin, L.M., V. Carter, F.C. Golet, and E.T. LaRoe. 1979. Classification of Wetlands and Deepwater Habitats of the United States. U.S. Department of the Interior, Fish and Wildlife Service, Washington, DC. FWS/OBS–79/31.

Dahl, T.E. 2005. Florida's Wetlands—An Update on Status and Trends 1985 to 1996. U.S. Department of Interior, Fish and Wildlife Service, Washington, D.C. 80 p.

Dahl, T.E. 2004. Remote Sensing as a Tool for Monitoring Wetland Habitat Change. *In*: Aguirre-Bravo, Celedonio, and others. Eds. 2004. Monitoring Science and Technology Symposium: Unifying Knowledge for Sustainability in the Western Hemisphere; 2004 September 20–24; Denver, CO. Proceedings RMRS–P–000. Ogden, UT: U.S. Department of Agriculture, Forest Service, Rocky Mountain Research Station.

Dahl, T.E. 2000. Status and trends of wetlands in conterminous United States 1986 to 1997. U.S. Department of the Interior, Fish and Wildlife Service, Washington, D.C. 82 p.

Dahl, T.E. 1990 a. Techniques for conducting variable intensity wetland inventories. *In* Convention on Wetlands of International Importance Especially as Waterfowl Habitat, Fourth Meeting of the Conference of the Contracting Parties, Montreux, Switzerland, Proceedings of Technical Workshop E.

Dahl, T.E. 1990 b. Wetland losses in the United States 1780's to 1980's. U.S. Department of the Interior, Fish and Wildlife Service, Washington, D.C. 13 p.

Dahl, T.E. and C.E. Johnson. 1991. Status and trends of wetlands in the conterminous United States, mid-1970s to mid-1980s. U.S. Department of the Interior. U.S. Fish and Wildlife Service, Washington, D.C. 28 p.

Dechka. J.A., S.E. Franklin. M.D. Watmough. R.P. Bennett and D.W. Ingstrup. 2002. Classification of wetland habitat and vegetation communities using multi-temporal Ikonos imagery in southern Saskatchewan. Can. J. Remote Sensing, Vol. 28. No. 5, pp. 679–685.

Environmental Defense Fund and World Wildlife Fund. 1992. How Wet is a Wetland? The Impacts of the Proposed Revisions to the Federal Wetlands Delineation Manual, New York, NY and Washington, D.C.

FAO. 1987. 1948-1985 World Crop and Livestock Statistics (Rome: 1987); FAO, FAOSTATS *Statistics Database*, updated 28 May 2002; FAO, *Yearbook of Fishery Statistics: Capture Production and Aquaculture Production* (various years).

Fisheries and Water Resources Policy Committee. 2004. The National Fish Habitat Initiative, Presented to the International Association of Fish and Wildlife Agencies.

Frayer, W.E., T.J. Monahan, D.C. Bowden, and F.A. Graybill. 1983. Status and trends of wetlands and deepwater habitats in the conterminous United States, 1950's to 1970's. Colorado State University, Fort Collins, CO. 31 p.

Gwin, S.E., M.E. Kentula and P.W. Shaffer. Evaluating the effects of wetland regulation through hydrogeomorphic classification and landscape profiles. Wetlands, Vol. 19, No. 3. pp. 477–489

Hammond, E.H. 1970. Physical subdivisions of the United States of America. *In*: U.S. Geological Survey. National atlas of the United States of America. Department of the Interior, Washington, D.C. 61 p.

Hefner, J.M. 1986. Wetlands of Florida 1950s to 1970s. *In*: Estevez, E.D., J. Miller, J. Morris and R. Hamman (eds.). Managing Cumulative Effects in Florida Wetlands. New College Environmental Studies Program Publication No 37. Omnipress, Madison, WI. pp. 23–31.

Kennish, M.J. 2004. Estuarine Research, Monitoring, and Resource Protection. CRC Press, Boca Raton, FL. 297 p.

Kentula, M.E., R.P. Brooks, S.E. Gwin, C.C. Holland, A.D. Sherman and J.C. Sifneos. 1993. An Approach to Imparving Decision Making in Wetland Restoration and Creation. Edited by A.J. Hairston. U.S. Environmental Protection Agency, Environmental Research Laboratory, Corvallis, OR. 151 p.

Kushlan, J.A., M.J. Steinkamp, K.C. Parsons, J. Capp, M. Acosta Cruz, M. Coulter, I Davidson, L. Dickson, N. Edelson, R. Elliot, M Erwin, S. Hatch, S. Kress, R. Milko, S. Miller, K. Mills, R. Paul, R. Phillips, J.E. Saliva, B. Sydeman, J. Trapp, J. Wheeler, and K. Wahl. 2002. Waterbird Conservation for the Americas: The North American Waterbird Conservation Plan, Version 1. Waterbird Conservation for the Americas, Washington, D.C. 78 p.

Langbein, W.B. and K.T. Iseri. 1960. General introduction and hydrologic definitions manual of hydrology. Part 1. General surface water techniques. U.S. Geological Survey, Water Supply Paper 1541–A. 29 p.

Lewis, J. 2005. Pond Ecology. Yale-New Haven Institute. New Haven, CT.

Lillesand, T.M. and R.W. Kieffer. 1987. Remote Sensing and Image Interpretation 2nd edition. John Wiley and Sons, N.Y. 721 p.

Louisiana Geological Survey and Environmental Protection Agency. 1987. Saving Louisiana's coastal wetlands: the need for a long-term plan of action. U.S. Environmental Protection Agency, EPA–230–02–87–026. Washington D.C.

Louisiana State University. 2005. Louisiana Coastal Issues. *www. publichealth.hurricane.lsu.edu.*

Mitsch, W.J. and J.G. Gosselink. 1993. Wetlands (2nd edition). Van Norstrand Reinhold, New York, NY. 722 p.

Moorman, T. 2005. America's Marsh. Ducks Unlimited, Southern Regional Office, Jackson, MS. 6 p.

National Marine Fisheries Service. 2004. Fisheries of the United States—2003, National Oceanic and Atmospheric Administration, National Marine Fisheries Service. Preliminary Report.

National Oceanic and Atmospheric Administration. 2001. Wetlands and fish: Catch the link. National Marine Fisheries Service, Office of Habitat Conservation, Silver Spring, MD. 48 p.

National Research Council. 1995. Wetlands: Characteristics and boundaries. Committee on Characterization of Wetlands, Water Science and Technology Board. National Academy Press, Washington, D.C. 268 p.

Ney, John J. and Louis A. Helfrich. 2003. Sustaining America's aquatic biodiversity—selected freshwater fish families. Virginia Polytechnic Institute and State University, Dept of Fisheries and Wildlife Sciences. Pub. No. 420–526.

Odum, W.E. and C.C. McIvor. 1990. Mangroves. *In*. R.L. Myers and J.J. Ewel (*eds.*). Ecosystems of Florida. University of Central Florida Press, Orlando. pp. 517–548.

Orth, R.J., K.A. Moore and J.F. Nowak. 1990. Monitoring Seagrass distribution and abundance patterns: A case study from the Chesapeake Bay. *In:* S.J. Kiraly, F.A. Cross and J.D. Buffington (eds.). Federal coastal wetland mapping programs. Biol. Rept. 90 (18). Fish and Wildlife Service, Washington, D.C. pp. 111–123.

Philipson, W. (editor) 1996. *Manual of Photographic Interpretation* (Second edition). American Society for Photogrammetry and Remote Sensing. Bethesda, MD

Patience, N. and V. Klemas. 1993. Wetland Functional health assessment using remote sensing and other techniques: Literature search. U.S. Department of Commerce, National Oceanic and Atmospheric Administration, National Marine Fisheries Service, SE Fisheries Science Center, Beaufort Laboratory, Beaufort, NC. 60 p.

Reed, P.B.1988. National list of plant species that occur in wetlands: 1988 National Summary. Biol. Rept. 88 (24). U.S. Fish and Wildlife Service, Washington, D.C. 244 p.

Sarndal, C-E., B. Swensson and J. Wretman. 1992. Model assisted survey sampling. Springer-Verlag, New York, NY.

Shaw, S.P. and C G. Fredine. 1956. Wetlands of the United States. Circular 39, Department of the Interior, Fish and Wildlife Service, Washington, D.C. 67 p.

Spalding, M.D., F. Blasco and C.D. Field (*eds.*). 1997. World Mangrove Atlas. The International Soc. for Mangrove Ecosystems, Okinawa, Japan. 178 p.

Taylor, A.K., P. Sprott and F. J. Mazzotti. 2002. The vital link between land and water: The importance of uplands for protecting wetland functions. Wildlife Ecology and Conservation Department, University of Florida, Florida Cooperative Extension Service, Institute of Food and Agricultural Sciences, University of Florida, Gainesville, FL. WEC45.

The Conservation Foundation. 1988. Protecting America's wetlands: an action agenda. Final Report of the National Wetlands Policy Forum. Washington, D.C. 69 p.

Thompson, S.K. 1992. Sampling. John Wiley and Sons, Inc., New York, NY.

Tiner, R.W. 1996. Wetlands, *In*: Manual of Photographic Interpretation, second edition. American Society for Photogrammetry and Remote Sensing, Falls Church, VA. 2440 p.

Tiner, R.W. 1990. Use of high-altitude aerial photography for inventorying forested wetlands in the United States. Forest Ecology and Management, 33/34: 593–604.

Tiner, R.W. Jr. 1984. Wetlands of the United States: Current status and recent trends. Department of the Interior. U.S. Fish and Wildlife Service. Washington, D.C. 59 p.

Tulane University. 2004. Louisiana coastal Land *Loss@www.tulane. edu*

U.S. Department of Agriculture. 1991. Hydric Soils of the United States. Soil Conservation Service, Miscellaneous Publication Number 1491, Washington, D.C.

U.S. Department of Agriculture. 1975. Soil taxonomy: A basic system of soil classification for making and interpreting soil surveys. U.S. Department of Agriculture. Soil Conservation Service, Soil Survey Staff, Agricultural Handbook 436, Washington, D.C. 754 p.

U.S. Department of Agriculture, Economic Research Service. 2005. The economics of food, farming, natural resources and rural America. Aquaculture: overview. U.S. Department of Agriculture, Washington, D.C.

U.S. Department of Agriculture, Natural Resources Conservation Service. 2004. National Resources Inventory Annual Report, 2004. U.S. Department of Agriculture, Washington, D.C.

U.S. Environmental Protection Agency. 1993. Management measures for protection of wetlands and riparian areas. *In*: Guidance Specifying Management Measures for Sources of Non-point Pollution in Coastal Waters. U.S. Environmental Protection Agency, Washington, D.C.

U.S. Environmental Protection Agency. 1999. Ecological Condition of Estuaries in the Gulf of Mexico. EPA 620–R–98–004. U.S. Environmental Protection Agency, Office of Research and Development, National Health and Environmental Effects Research Laboratory, Gulf Ecology Division, Gulf Breeze, FL. 71 p.

U.S. Environmental Protection Agency. 2004. National Coastal Condition Report II. Office of Research and Development/Office of Water Washington, D.C. EPA–620/R–03/002

U.S. Fish and Wildlife Service. 2004a. Conserving America's Fisheries. Department of the Interior, Fish and Wildlife Service, Washington, D.C. 24 p.

U.S. Fish and Wildlife Service. 2004b. Technical Procedures for Wetlands Status and Trends. Branch of Habitat Assessment, Arlington, VA. 62 p.

U.S. Fish and Wildlife Service. 2001. National Survey of Fishing, Hunting, and Wildlife-Associated Recreation. Department of the Interior, Fish and Wildlife Service, Washington, D.C.

U.S. Fish and Wildlife Service. 1996. The South Florida Ecosystem. U.S. Fish and Wildlife Service—South Florida Ecosystem Office, Vero Beach, FL. 45 p. plus Appendices.

U.S. Fish and Wildlife Service. 1994a. Continuous wetlands trend analysis project specifications (photo-interpretation and cartographic procedures). Wetland Status and Trends, Branch of Habitat Assessment, Fish and Wildlife Service, Washington, D.C. 60 p.

U.S. Fish and Wildlife Service. 1994b. Technical specifications and protocols for Status and Trends digital files. Wetland Status and Trends, Branch of Habitat Assessment, Fish and Wildlife Service, Washington, D.C. 35 p. plus appendices.

U.S. Geological Survey. 2005 a. USGS reports new wetland loss from Hurricane Katrina in Southeastern Louisiana. Department of the Interior, U.S. Geological Survey. News Release, Sept. 14, 2005.

U.S. Geological Survey, 2005 b. Aerial photography of post Hurricane Katrina. *www.lacoast.gov.* National Wetlands Research Center, Lafayette, LA.

Watmough, M.D., D.W. Ingstrup, D.C. Duncan and H.J. Schinke. 2002. Prairie Habitat Joint Venture Habitat Monitoring Program Phase 1: Recent habitat trends in NAWMP targeted landscapes. Technical Report Series No. 391, Canadian Wildlife Service, Edmonton, Alberta, Canada. 93 p.

Weber, M.L. 1995. Healthy coasts, healthy economy: A national overview of America's coasts. Technical Report, Coast Alliance, Washington, D.C.

Williams, S.J. 1995. Louisiana coastal wetlands: A resource at risk. U.S, Geological Survey, Marine and Coastal Geology Program, Reston, VA.

Williams, Z., Z.S. Pinson, R.P. Stumpf and E.A. Raabe. 1995. Sea-level rise and coastal forests on the Gulf of Mexico. Department of the Interior, U.S. Geological Survey. Open-File Report 99–441. 87 p.

Zinn, J.A. and C. Copeland. 2002. Wetland Issues. Issue Brief for Congress—Resources, Science and Industry Division, Congressional Research Service, The Library of Congress IB97014. 15 p.

Acknowledgement of Cooperators

The Fish and Wildlife Service is indebted to the following agencies and organizations who have provided services, expertise and assistance over the course of this study.

Florida Resource and Environmental Analysis Center
Florida State University
Tallahassee, Florida

Space Imaging Corporation
Thornton, Colorado

Digital Globe Corporation
Longmont, Colorado 80503

Eastern Geographic Science Center
Advanced Systems Center
U.S. Geological Survey
Reston, Virginia

Commercial Partnerships Team
U.S. Geological Survey
Rolla, Missouri

Office of Water Information
U.S. Geological Survey
Madison, Wisconsin

The National Map
U.S. Geological Survey
Reston, Virginia

Aeromap Corporation
Anchorage, Alaska

St. Mary's University
Geospatial Services Dept.
Winona, Minnesota

South Dakota State University
Department of Wildlife and Fisheries
Brookings, South Dakota

Natural Resources Assessment Group
University of Massachusetts
Department of Plant & Soil Sciences
Amherst, Massachusetts.

U. S. Fish and Wildlife Service
Region 6 HAPET Office
Bismarck, North Dakota

Indiana Department of Environmental Management
Indianapolis, Indiana

Colorado State University
Fort Collins, Colorado

Minnesota Land Management Information System
Minnesota Geographic Data Clearinghouse
St. Paul, Minnesota

Minnesota Pollution Control Agency—Biological Monitoring Unit
Environmental Outcomes Division
St. Paul, Minnesota

Minnesota Department of Natural Resources
St. Paul, Minnesota

Minnesota Board of Water and Soil Resources
St. Paul, Minnesota

Canadian Wildlife Service
Environmental Conservation Branch
Prairie and Northern Region
Edmonton, Alberta
Canada

Office of Science
U.S. Fish and Wildlife Service
Arlington, Virginia

Pheasants Forever
St. Paul, Minnesota

IzaakWalton League of America, Inc.
Gaithersburg, Maryland

Iowa Department of Natural Resources
Des Moines, Louisiana

Kansas Water Office
Topeka, Kansas

Oregon Department of State Lands
Salem, Oregon

Michigan Department of Environmental Quality
Lansing, Michigan

Natural Resource Conservation Service
U.S. Department of Agriculture
Washington, D.C.

U.S. Army Corps of Engineers
Washington, D.C.

U.S. Environmental Protection Agency
Washington, D.C.

National Oceanic and Atmospheric
Administration
National Marine Fisheries Service
Washington, D.C.

Office of Management and Budget
Washington, D.C.

U.S. Department of Agriculture
Farm Services Agency
Washington, D.C.

Association of State Wetland Managers
Windham, Maine

National Park Service—Cumberland Island
National Seashore, Georgia

Fishery Resources Office
U.S. Fish and Wildlife Service
Onalaska, Wisconsin

Upper Mississippi River National Wildlife and Fish
Refuge—La Crosse District
U.S. Fish and Wildlife Service
Onalaska, Wisconsin

Chincoteague National Wildlife Refuge
U.S. Fish and Wildlife Service
Chincoteague Island, Virginia

Back Bay National Wildlife Refuge
U.S. Fish and Wildlife Service
Virginia Beach, Virginia

Edwin B. Forsythe National Wildlife Refuge
U.S. Fish and Wildlife Service
Oceanville, New Jersey

Mr. Justin Miner
SWCA Environmental Consultants
Portland, Oregon

Cypress Creek National Wildlife Refuge. Photo courtesy of the FWS.

A shrub bog in northern Wisconsin, 2005.

Appendix A.
Definitions of Habitat Categories Used by Status and Trends

Wetlands[1]

In general terms, wetlands are lands where saturation with water is the dominant factor determining the nature of soil development and the types of plant and animal communities living in the soil and on its surface. The single feature that most wetlands share is soil or substrate that is at least periodically saturated with or covered by water. The water creates severe physiological problems for all plants and animals except those that are adapted for life in water or in saturated soil.

> Wetlands are lands transitional between terrestrial and aquatic systems where the water table is usually at or near the surface or the land is covered by shallow water. For purposes of this classification wetlands must have one or more of the following three attributes: (1) at least periodically, the land supports predominantly hydrophytes,[2] (2) the substrate is predominantly undrained hydric soil,[3] and (3) the substrate is non-soil and is saturated with water or covered by shallow water at some time during the growing season of each year.

The term wetland includes a variety of areas that fall into one of five categories: (1) areas with hydrophytes and hydric soils, such as those commonly known as marshes, swamps, and bogs; (2) areas without hydrophytes but with hydric soils—for example, flats where drastic fluctuation in water level, wave action, turbidity, or high concentration of salts may prevent the growth of hydrophytes; (3) areas with hydrophytes but non-hydric soils, such as margins of impoundments or excavations where hydrophytes have become established but hydric soils have not yet developed; (4) areas without soils but with hydrophytes such as the seaweed-covered portions of rocky shores; and (5) wetlands without soil and without hydrophytes, such as gravel beaches or rocky shores without vegetation.

Marine System
The marine system consists of the open ocean overlying the continental shelf and its associated high energy coastline. Marine habitats are exposed to the waves and currents of the open ocean. Salinity exceeds 30 parts per thousand, with little or no dilution except outside the mouths of estuaries. Shallow coastal indentations or bays without appreciable freshwater inflow and coasts with exposed rocky islands that provide the mainland with little or no shelter from wind and waves, are also considered part of the Marine System because they generally support typical marine biota.

Estuarine System
The estuarine system consists of deepwater tidal habitats and adjacent tidal wetlands that are usually semi-enclosed by land but have open, partly obstructed, or sporadic access to the open ocean, and in which ocean water is at least occasionally diluted by freshwater runoff from the land. The salinity may be periodically increased above that of the open ocean by evaporation. Along some low energy coastlines there is appreciable dilution of sea water. Offshore areas with typical estuarine plants and animals, such as red mangroves (*Rhizophora mangle*)

---

[1] Adapted from Cowardin *et al*. 1979.

[2] The U.S. Fish and Wildlife Service has published the list of plant species that occur in wetlands of the United States (Reed 1988).

[3] The U.S. Department of Agriculture has developed the list of hydric soils for the United States (U.S. Department of Agriculture 1991).

and eastern oysters (*Crassostrea virginica*), are also included in the Estuarine System.

Marine and Estuarine Subsystems

Subtidal   The substrate is continuously submerged by marine or estuarine waters.

Intertidal   The substrate is exposed and flooded by tides. Intertidal includes the splash zone of coastal waters.

Palustrine System   The palustrine (freshwater) system includes all non-tidal wetlands dominated by trees, shrubs, persistent emergents, emergent mosses or lichens, farmed wetlands, and all such wetlands that occur in tidal areas where salinity due to ocean-derived salts is below 0.5 parts per thousand. It also includes wetlands lacking such vegetation, but with all of the following four characteristics: (1) area less than 20 acres (8 ha); (2) an active wave formed or bedrock shoreline features are lacking; (3) water depth in the deepest part of basin less than 6.6 feet (2 meters) at low water; and (4) salinity due to ocean derived salts less than 0.5 parts per thousand.

Classes

Unconsolidated Bottom   Unconsolidated bottom includes all wetlands with at least 25 percent cover of particles smaller than stones, and a vegetative cover less than 30 percent. Examples of unconsolidated substrates are: sand, mud, organic material, cobble gravel.

Aquatic Bed   Aquatic beds are dominated by plants that grow principally on or below the surface of the water for most of the growing season in most years. Examples include seagrass beds, pondweeds (*Potamogeton spp.*), wild celery (*Vallisneria americana*), watereed (*Elodea spp.*), and duckweed (*Lemna spp.*).

Rocky Shore   Rocky shore includes all wetland environments characterized by bedrock, stones, or boulders which singly or in combination have an areal cover of 75 percent or more and an areal vegetative coverage of less than 30 percent.

Unconsolidated Shore   Unconsolidated shore includes all wetland habitats having two characteristics: (1) unconsolidated substrates with less than 75 percent areal cover of stones, boulders or bedrock and; (2) less than 30 percent areal cover of vegetation other than pioneering plants.

Emergent Wetland   Emergent wetlands are characterized by erect, rooted, herbaceous hydrophytes, excluding mosses and lichens. This vegetation is present for most of the growing season in most years. These wetlands are usually dominated by perennial plants.

Shrub Wetland   Shrub wetlands include areas dominated by woody vegetation less than 20 feet (6 meters) tall. The species include true shrubs, young trees, and trees or shrubs that are small or stunted because of environmental conditions.

Forested Wetland	Forested wetlands are characterized by woody vegetation that is 20 feet (6 meters) tall or taller.
Farmed Wetland	Farmed wetlands are wetlands that meet the Cowardin *et al.* definition where the soil surface has been mechanically or physically altered for production of crops, but where hydrophytes will become reestablished if farming is discontinued.

Deepwater Habitats

Wetlands and deepwater habitats are defined separately because the term wetland has not included deep permanent water bodies. For conducting status and trends studies, Riverine and Lacustrine were considered deepwater habitats. Elements of Marine or Estuarine systems can be wetland or deepwater. Palustrine includes only wetland habitats.

Deepwater habitats are permanently flooded land lying below the deepwater boundary of wetlands. Deepwater habitats include environments where surface water is permanent and often deep, so that water, rather than air, is the principal medium in which the dominant organisms live, whether or not they are attached to the substrate. As in wetlands, the dominant plants were hydrophytes; however, the substrates were considered non-soil because the water is too deep to support emergent vegetation (U.S. Department of Agriculture 1975).

Riverine System	The riverine system includes deepwater habitats contained within a channel, with the exception of habitats with water containing ocean derived salts in excess of 0.5 parts per thousand. A channel is "an open conduit either naturally or artificially created which periodically or continuously contains moving water, or which forms a connecting link between two bodies of standing water" (Langbein and Iseri 1960).
Lacustrine System	The lacustrine system includes deepwater habitats with all of the following characteristics: (1) situated in a topographic depression or a dammed river channel; (2) lacking trees, shrubs, persistent emergents, emergent mosses or lichens with greater than 30 percent coverage; (3) total area exceeds 20 acres (8 ha).

Uplands

Agriculture[4]	Agricultural land may be defined broadly as land used primarily for production of food and fiber. Agricultural activity is evidenced by distinctive geometric field and road patterns on the landscape and the traces produced by livestock or mechanized equipment. Examples of agricultural land use include cropland and pasture; orchards, groves, vineyards, nurseries, cultivated lands, and ornamental horticultural areas including sod farms; confined feeding operations; and other agricultural land including livestock feed lots, farmsteads including houses, support structures (silos) and adjacent yards, barns, poultry sheds, etc.
Urban	Urban land is comprised of areas of intensive use in which much of the land is covered by structures (high building density). Urbanized areas are cities and towns that provide the goods and services needed to survive by modern day standards through a central business district. Services such as banking, medical and legal office buildings,

---

[4] Adapted from Anderson *et al.* 1976.

supermarkets, and department stores make up the business center of a city. Commercial strip developments along main transportation routes, shopping centers, contiguous dense residential areas, industrial and commercial complexes, transportation, power and communication facilities, city parks, ball fields and golf courses can also be included in the urban category.

Forested Plantation

Forested plantations include areas of planted and managed forest stands. Planted pines, Christmas tree farms, clear cuts, and other managed forest stands, such as hardwood forestry are included in this category. Forested plantations can be identified by observing the following remote sensing indicators: 1) trees planted in rows or blocks; 2) forested blocks growing with uniform crown heights; and 3) logging activity and use patterns.

Rural Development

Rural developments occur in sparse rural and suburban settings outside distinct urban cities and towns. They are characterized by non-intensive land use and sparse building density. Typically, a rural development is a cross-roads community that has a corner gas station and a convenience store which are surrounded by sparse residential housing and agriculture. Scattered suburban communities located outside of a major urban center can also be included in this category as well as some industrial and commercial complexes; isolated transportation, power, and communication facilities; strip mines; quarries; and recreational areas such as golf courses, etc. Major highways through rural development areas are included in the rural development category.

Other Land Use

Other land use is composed of uplands not characterized by the previous categories. Typically these lands would include native prairie; unmanaged or non-patterned upland forests, conservation lands and scrub lands; and barren land. Lands in transition may also fit into this category. Transitional lands are lands in transition from one land use to another. They generally occur in large acreage blocks of 40 acres (16 ha) or more and are characterized by the lack of any remote sensor information that would enable the interpreter to reliably predict future use. The transitional phase occurs when wetlands are drained, ditched, filled, leveled, or the vegetation has been removed and the area is temporarily bare.

Appendix B.
Hammond (1970) Physiographic Regions of the United States

1	Coast Ranges
2	Puget Willamette Lowland
3	Cascade Klamath Sierra Nevada Ranges
4	Central Valley of California
5	Columbia Basin
6	Blue Mountains
7	Harney and Owyhee Broken Lands
8	Basin and Range Area
9	Northern Rocky Mountains
10	Snake River Lowland
11	Middle Rocky Mountains
12	Wyoming Big Horn Basins
13	Colorado River Plateaus
14	Upper Gila Mountains
15	North Central Lake Swamp Moraine Plains
16	Upper Missouri Basin Broken Lands
17	Southern Rocky Mountains
18	Rocky Mountain Piedmont
19	High Plains
20	Stockton Balcones Escarpment
21	Dakota Minnesota Drift and Lake Bed Flats
22	Nebraska Sand Hills
23	West Central Rolling Hills
24	Midcontinent Plains and Escarpments
25	Southwest Wisconsin Hills
26	Middle Western Upland Plain
27	Ozark Ouachita Highlands
28	Lower Mississippi Alluvial Plain
29	East Central Drift and Lake Bed Flats
30	Eastern Interior Uplands and Basins
31	Appalachian Highlands
32	Adirondack New England Highlands
33	Lower New England
34	Gulf Atlantic Rolling Plain
35	Gulf Atlantic Coastal Flats
36	Coastal Zone

Appendix C.

This table presents estimates of acreage by classification and the number of acres that changed classification between 1998 and 2004. The rows identify the 2004 classification. The columns identify the classification and acreage of 1998. The number under the acreage estimate for each entry is the percentage coefficient variation for that estimate.

| | | | | | 1998 Classification | | | | | |
| | | **Saltwater Habitats** | | | | | | | **Freshwater** | | |
		Marine Subtidal	Marine Intertidal	Estuarine Subtidal	Estuarine Aquatic Bed	Estuarine Emergents	Estuarine Forested Shrub	Estuarine Unconsolidated Shore	Palustrine Aquatic Bed	Palustrine Emergents	Palustrine Forested
Saltwater Habitats	Marine Subtidal	2178861 / 32	499 / 62	0 / —	0 / —	191 / 95	0 / —	57 / 68	0 / —	0 / —	0 / —
	Marine Intertidal	4240 / 44	125534 / 21	181 / 73	0 / —	0 / —	18 / 95	297 / 62	0 / —	0 / —	0 / —
	Estuarine Subtidal	262 / 61	201 / 48	17634884 / 2	873 / 95	19548 / 39	424 / 91	20049 / 24	0 / —	6 / 97	0 / —
	Estuarine Aquatic Bed	0 / —	0 / —	0 / —	30849 / 27	0 / —	0 / —	0 / —	0 / —	0 / —	0 / —
	Estuarine Emergents	739 / 47	1428 / 41	48856 / 12	319 / 72	3861358 / 4	1590 / 43	5882 / 34	0 / —	139 / 89	0 / —
	Estuarine Forested Shrub	88 / 95	23 / 77	630 / 29	0 / —	0 / —	679255 / 13	986 / 52	0 / —	0 / —	0 / —
	Estuarine Unconsolidated Shore	300 / 56	285 / 52	19468 / 45	0 / —	2768 / 35	293 / 55	539881 / 11	0 / —	0 / —	0 / —
Freshwater Habitats	Palustrine Aquatic Bed	0 / —	0 / —	0 / —	0 / —	0 / —	0 / —	0 / —	240385 / 12	12429 / 34	55 / 99
	Palustrine Emergents	0 / —	0 / —	1408 / 47	376 / 100	1636 / 73	0 / —	90 / 92	24645 / 44	24661561 / 8	173402 / 16
	Palustrine Forested	0 / —	0 / —	53 / 80	0 / —	895 / 103	0 / —	0 / —	4081 / 57	387948 / 13	49246357 / 3
	Palustrine Shrub	0 / —	0 / —	93 / 95	0 / —	9 / 95	476 / 95	131 / 95	1172 / 47	408394 / 17	2596759 / 8
	Palustrine Unconsolidated Bottom	0 / —	0 / —	0 / —	0 / —	0 / —	0 / —	0 / —	8560 / 31	138847 / 15	2009 / 50
	Palustrine Unconsolidated Shore	0 / —	0 / —	0 / —	0 / —	0 / —	0 / —	0 / —	0 / —	3799 / 51	241 / 81
Deepwater Habitats	Lacustrine	0 / —	0 / —	8246 / 66	0 / —	2036 / 96	0 / —	33 / 95	2084 / 87	167452 / 43	0 / —
	Riverine	0 / —	0 / —	463 / 89	0 / —	0 / —	0 / —	0 / —	0 / —	14312 / 49	2129 / 79
Uplands	Agriculture	0 / —	0 / —	30 / 51	19 / 104	155 / 104	0 / —	0 / —	3558 / 43	216018 / 23	2999 / 64
	Urban	0 / —	0 / —	1604 / 66	0 / —	74 / 73	0 / —	0 / —	12 / 98	896 / 49	185 / 99
	Upland Forested Plantation	0 / —	0 / —	0 / —	0 / —	0 / —	0 / —	0 / —	202 / 100	2331 / 45	8 / 98
	Upland Rural Development	0 / —	0 / —	56 / 84	0 / —	0 / —	0 / —	0 / —	0 / —	6297 / 61	489 / 100
	Other	121 / 62	606 / 54	2852 / 38	0 / —	867 / 53	142 / 65	171 / 51	6183 / 64	131560 / 37	6732 / 39
Acreage Totals, 2004		2184611 / 32	128577 / 20	17717824 / 2	32436 / 26	3889536 / 4	682197 / 12	567531 / 10	290880 / 11	26146988 / 8	52081364 / 3

(Left vertical axis label: 2004 Classification, Estimated Acreage and Percent Coefficient of Variation)

and Acreage

	Habitats			Deepwater Habitats		Uplands						
Palustrine Shrub	Palustrine Unconsolidated Bottom	Palustrine Unconsolidated Shore	Lacustrine	Riverine	Agriculture	Urban	Upland Forested Plantation	Upland Rural Development	Other	Acreage Totals, 1996	
0 —	0 —	0 —	0 —	0 —	0 —	0 —	0 —	0 —	0 —	2179608 32	Marine Subtidal
0 —	0 —	0 —	0 —	0 —	0 —	0 —	0 —	17 94	163 95	130449 20	Marine Intertidal
0 —	75 62	224 94	1690 95	0 —	0 —	1511 68	0 —	3 95	780 59	17680580 2	Estuarine Subtidal
0 —	0 —	0 —	0 —	0 —	0 —	0 —	0 —	0 —	0 —	30849 27	Estuarine Aquatic Bed
10 95	83 53	3 95	0 —	33 94	0 —	1489 54	0 —	94 50	1245 44	3922768 4	Estuarine Emergents
0 —	45 70	0 —	0 —	0 —	0 —	67 58	0 —	330 85	18 95	681392 12	Estuarine Forested Shrub
63 95	3 96	24 94	30 95	0 —	0 —	47 75	0 —	72 84	0 —	563285 11	Estuarine Unconsolidated Shore
1955 83	9199 35	0 —	378 58	1627 99	852 60	268 68	0 —	93 59	197 100	267438 12	Palustrine Aquatic Bed
639172 12	151138 31	1489 43	230166 28	6673 33	330434 19	23947 29	19141 30	18648 27	5630 26	26289557 8	Palustrine Emergents
1446340 15	60318 25	865 45	5424 54	21282 49	103237 45	64901 25	23211 31	84521 29	33705 29	51483138 3	Palustrine Forested
15392857 4	30642 19	1303 57	10857 41	0 —	59492 32	22472 28	0 —	16685 22	6361 29	18542204 4	Palustrine Shrub
18354 23	4989715 4	4321 30	14027 47	16985 70	28489 17	12467 19	1120 54	16332 24	15595 20	5266822 4	Palustrine Unconsolidated Bottom
1351 55	9825 41	362130 17	2385 99	0 —	1001 46	333 58	118 81	1026 51	2197 55	384405 16	Palustrine Unconsolidated Shore
35656 77	1110 52	5892 87	16364215 10	4552 97	2543 56	527 63	0 —	10331 88	5834 66	16610509 10	Lacustrine
38043 33	4423 80	0 —	184 84	6696806 9	188 85	106 100	0 —	85 98	8782 59	6765520 9	Riverine
43040 54	315332 9	13091 40	59372 35	11862 38							Agriculture
6 95	35526 31	335 94	1689 50	73 98							Urban
375 71	21302 21	1304 84	9401 94	0 —							Upland Forested Plantation
1008 96	77853 42	764 53	6562 40	1351 90							Upland Rural Development
23706 54	232206 10	1254 41	67027 40	52024 37							Other
17641435 4	5938765 4	404300 16	16773407 10	6813268 9							Acreage Totals, 2004

Appendix D.
Representative Wetland Restoration Programs and Activities

Within the Federal Government, there exist a number of agencies and organizations working to restore aquatic habitats and values they provide to society. The number of stream, river, lake, wetland and estuary restoration projects is steadily increasing. Current federal initiatives call for a wide range of restoration actions, including improving or restoring stream corridors, elimination of invasive species, and restoration (re-establishment) of wetland area and functions. Some of the prominent federal agencies and programs that conduct wetland restoration are listed below.[1]

Key Federal Agencies

Department of the Interior

U.S. Fish and Wildlife Service

Partners for Fish and Wildlife Program
Coastal Program
National Wildlife Refuge System
North American Wetlands Conservation Program
National Coastal Wetlands Grant Program
Fish and Wildlife Management Assistance
Fisheries Resource Program
North American Waterfowl Management Plan
Federal Duck Stamp Program
Office of Migratory Bird Management
Jobs in the Woods Watershed Restoration Program
Endangered Species Recovery Program
The Natural Resource Damage Assessment and Restoration Program
Wildlife and Sport Fish Restoration Programs, Division of Federal Assistance
    The Federal Aid in Wildlife Restoration Act (Pittman-Robertson Act)
    The Federal Aid in Sport Fish Restoration Act (Dingell-Johnson Act)

National Park Service

National Park Service Exotic Plant Management Program
Wetlands Program

Bureau of Land Management

Land Acquisition Program
Interior Columbia Basin Ecosystem Management Project
Riparian Conservation Areas Program
PACFISH and INFISH Programs

Bureau of Reclamation

Stream Corridor Restoration
Resource Management and Planning

---

[1] Partial listing

Geological Survey

Water Program
  National Water Quality Assessment Program (NAWQA)
Biological Resources Program

U.S. Environmental Protection Agency

Clean Water Act State Revolving Fund
Five-Star Restoration Program
Non-point Source Implementation Grants (319 Program)
National Estuary Program
EPA Community-Based Environmental Protection
Wetland Grants Program
Clean Water Act Program

U.S. Department of Agriculture

Forest Service

Northwest Forest Plan
Taking Wing Program
Wetlands Management Programs
Land Acquisition Program

Natural Resources Conservation Service

Wetlands Reserve Program
Conservation Technical Assistance Program
Emergency Watershed Protection Program
Environmental Quality Incentives Program
Watershed Protection and Flood Prevention Program
Wildlife Habitat Incentives Program
Farm and Ranchlands Protection Program
Grasslands Reserve Program

Farm Services Agency

Conservation Reserve Program

U.S. Department of Commerce

National Oceanic and Atmospheric Administration

Coastal Zone Management Program
National Marine Estuarine Reserve System
Community Based Restoration Program
Great Lakes Restoration Program
Coastal and Estuarine Land Conservation Program
Sea Grant Program
Damage Assessment and Restoration Program

National Marine Fisheries Service

Office of Habitat Assessment Programs

U.S. Department of Defense

Interservice Environmental Education Review Board
Conservation Programs on Military Reservations
Cooperative agreements for land management on Department of Defense installations
Natural resources and fish and wildlife management on military reservations

Department of the Army

Conservation Assistance Program
Ecosystem Management Program
Fish and Wildlife Conservation Program

U.S. Army Corps of Engineers

Ecosystem Management and Restoration Research Program
Aquatic Ecosystem Restoration Program
Clean Water Act Program
Hamilton Airfield (CA) Wetlands Restoration Project

Department of the Navy

Environmental Restoration Programs
Management of Natural Resources on Naval Bases

U.S. Marine Corps

Environmental Compliance Evaluation Program
The Defense Environmental Restoration Program

Department of the Air Force

Federal Facility Environmental Restoration Program
Base comprehensive planning activities

Department of Homeland Security

Federal Emergency Management Agencey

National Flood Mapping Program
National Flood Insurance Program

Department of Energy

Office of Environmental Management Program
Office of Science Biological and Environmental Research

Department of Transportation

Federal Aviation and Transit Programs

Federal Highway Administration

Federal Highway Administration Programs

Extra-Governmental Organizations

Coastal America

Comprehensive Everglades Restoration Plan

Tennessee Valley Authority

Louisiana Coastal Area Environmental Restoration

Federal Legislation, Directives or Other Mechanisms that Support Wetland Restoration

Surplus Federal Property Transfer
Migratory Bird Treaty
Endangered Species Act
Coastal Barrier Resources Act
Coastal Zone Management Act
Coastal Wetlands Planning, Protection, Restoration Act
Food Security Act
Clean Water Act
Fish and Wildlife Coordination Act
Water Resources Development Act
Interanl Revenue Code
National Environmental Policy Act
RAMSAR Treaty
Executive Order 11988
Executive Order 11990
Federal Aid in Sport Fish Restoration Act
Federal Aid in Wildlife Restoration Act
Land and Water Conservation Fund Act
North American Wetlands Conservation Act
Watershed Protection and Flood Prevention Act

Native American Tribes

Native American culture depends on healthy natural resources to support fishing and hunting. To protect their resources, tribes are developing various land conservation and aquatic resource restoration actions which consider the land uses, hydrology, and cultural issues for specific reservations.

Non-governmental Organizations with Active Wetland Restoration Programs or Partnerships[2]

American Fisheries Society

American Rivers

American Water Resources Association

Association of State Floodplain Managers

Association of State Wetland Managers

Bass Anglers Sportsman Society

Ducks Unlimited

Isaac Walton League of American

Trout Unlimited

National Association of Conservation Districts

National Association of Counties

National Association of Service and Conservation Corps

National Audobon Society

National Fish and Wildlife Foundation

Native Plant Society

National Wildlife Federation

Partners in Flight

Pheasants Forever

Restore America's Estuaries

River Network

State Waterfowl Associations

The Biodiversity Partnership

The Conservation Fund

The Nature Conservancy

The Sport Fishing and Boating Partnership Council

Wildlife Habitat Council

---

[2] Partial list.

www.ingramcontent.com/pod-product-compliance
Lightning Source LLC
Chambersburg PA
CBHW080306290526
45790CB00005B/1942